## The Cure for Spiritual HIV

# The Cure for Spiritual HIV

KBM MEDIA
*Hearts on fire, lives on purpose*

Grace With Blood On It: The Cure for Spiritual HIV
Foster Christy
ISBN No. 978-0-9819403-3-5
©2010 by Foster Christy. All rights reserved.

Published by KBM Media, a division of Kingdom Building Ministries,
14485 E. Evans Ave., Aurora, Colorado 80014.

Cover design by Meghan Locklair.

Scripture references from the Holy Bible, New International Version (NIV).
©1973, 1978, 1984, International Bible Society. Used by permission of Zondervan Bible
Publishers. Bold lettering indicates emphasis added by the authors.

Requests to use material contained in this publication should be sent in writing to:
Publisher, KBM Media, 14485 E. Evans Ave., Aurora, CO, 80014.

Visit us online at www.kbm.org.
For more about Foster Christy, visit www.fosterchristy.com.

# Table of Contents

# INTRODUCTION
## Memories of an Alabama Childhood

I GAVE MY LIFE TO CHRIST three weeks before I left Huntsville to play football for Auburn University. It was an intense time of life that brought into sharp focus the final stages of a strong-willed Alabama boy's storied athletic career. And while this season of life sparked a slow awakening to the riches I would one day experience in a life lived for God, I was at the time immature and unprepared to actually live that life out. At the time of my surrender to the person of Jesus Christ, my church involvement had been minimal.

I arrived at my late teens having achieved more athletic success than I'd ever imagined, but the sad fact was that I hadn't given Jesus much consideration. My interests lay elsewhere. Still, looking back, my sports background and church experience had a long-lasting impact. I couldn't have known how deeply the early childhood church experiences I *did* have would come to characterize how I would relate to Jesus, His Church, and His people as an adult.

That journey began in a typical American middle class neighborhood in Huntsville, Alabama. And this particular story begins with my dad. It was my father, in my backyard, who invested hours playing catch and hitting fly balls on sweaty, Deep South afternoons after school. It was my father who taught my brother and I how to play sports.

Dad was a NASA engineer who helped design the computer systems of the old Saturn and Apollo rockets. Though he wasn't particularly athletic himself, he was an extremely detailed engineer who flat-out knew how to do stuff. Those were the days when a roomful of refrigerator-sized, reel-to-reel computers had the same memory that an iPod does today and when men like my dad, from a post-Depression-era generation, stayed the course and worked hard, often for a single company their entire careers. That was my dad. He worked for NASA for nearly forty years, and when it came to physics or computers or building a short-wave radio from an old pipe and a couple of wires he found on the side of the road, he had a knack for figuring things out.

This translated incredibly well, as it happens, to coaching. With the same aptitude he used to design rockets, dad, through sheer dogged determination, taught himself how to diagram a game plan, swing a bat, or throw a knuckle ball or tight spiral.

As a kid, I'd see dad studying those old illustrated, black-and-white rulebooks on baseball, memorizing the rules, pouring through books and magazines on batting and training techniques. Then he'd take us out in the backyard and, step-by-step, teach my brother and I how to play. He wasn't a domineering, type-A parent by any means, yet through strict application of a sport's rules, techniques, and strategies, he became a legendary coach in the local southeast Huntsville leagues. Dad coached our undefeated YMCA football and baseball teams for years on end, and under his coaching I developed into one of the better pitchers in our Little League division.

By twelve, I was throwing the baseball—fastball, change-up, knuckle ball—well enough that when some of the other players heard I was pitching, they wouldn't show up. I remember those days well, and for a twelve-year-old, it was pretty heady stuff. But I have to give my dad much of the credit; he helped put me on solid footing athletically, instilling in me a strong work ethic and, ultimately, teaching me how to compete.

I'd begun to learn that if I worked hard and stayed dedicated, I probably had the physical gifts needed to carve out some kind of athletic career in football, baseball, or track. But while my family attended church, my actual church experiences in those days were passive and unfocused.

I have vivid memories singing as a child in Sunday school, reciting songs on a music sheet that helped us learn the books of the New Testament. And, looking back from the vantage of nearly thirty years in ministry, there's nothing wrong with singing songs in Sunday school.

But I remember seeing the men wearing suits and ties and the women all dressed up in hats and make-up, and wondering why. Why did we have to dress up to go to church? Today, I likewise profess that there's certainly nothing wrong with suits, ties, and people looking good in church. I can still hear the choir singing hymns and remember their robes and collars, the congregation standing at attention, thumbing through hymnals, searching for the right song. Again, nothing wrong with choirs and hymnals. The fact is, back then, I didn't connect going to church with saving faith, Christianity or, necessarily, even with God. It was just me going to church, simply one more thing to do at the end of the weekend.

But mostly I remember a week-after-week routine that seemed little more than a dry, boring exercise. I remember a sanctuary full of parishioners sitting stoically, like spectators at a movie, watching the minister lead us through a repetitive litany of steps and verses. Okay, I'll admit it: on the surface there's nothing wrong with thoughtful, carefully planned and orchestrated programs, order of service, or structure.

But aside from all of this, my most enduring memory of church was an empty and unsettling feeling—one that I once chalked up to my short teenage attention span. Sitting in church with a hundred or so other well-dressed, self-conscious Protestants, it felt to me like listening to a lecture in biology class. As a body, we constituted little more than a passive audience sitting quietly and orderly in pews, participating in a call-and-response service that, in hindsight, seemed scripted down to the minute. Perhaps it had all been designed to give the impression of authenticity, something meant to *feel* like genuine, Spirit-led worship. For me it always fell far short—so much so that, even as a young, distracted kid, I couldn't help asking myself: *What's the point?*

I will say this, in that seemingly staged environment, my self-absorbed teenage heart was not drawn to God. From my standpoint, He was nowhere to be found. Neither His Spirit nor the sense of His presence became evident to me. Not that I was looking for it. Yet, looking around, God seemed to me impossibly distant and abstract. If He existed at all, I found Him utterly unknowable. Subsequently, my youthful impressions of church were visions of stiff formality and rigid programs rather than that of being ushered into an intimate *familiarity* with the very One we were supposed to be worshipping. Services seemed anchored to a script and timed to the minute so that congregants wouldn't get restless and want to escape in time to catch the Sunday lunch special. They rarely provided a place or time to simply linger before the Lord, rest in Him, deeply worship or, simply, pray. Looking back, I can't recall meeting many who, by their words and deeds, either taught or demonstrated what it was to know or walk intimately with God. Maybe I was looking for someone to show me what it was to truly taste and see, through their own life, that He was in fact *good.*

Yes, I was a churchgoer in a strict definition of the term. But I do not feel I ever really experienced Jesus. I don't recall hearing the gospel presented in a way that truly convicted me of my sin so as to lead me to repentance. I don't recall ever really hearing about the Jesus of the New Testament or why I needed Him.

In time, I ended up going to church for other reasons: to see my friends and, sometime later, my girlfriend. It sure wasn't to meet or fellowship with the God of the universe. Far from being to me the awesome Lord of all creativity, redemption, and purpose, God became (to a young, budding, girl-obsessed athlete) little more than a ritual that I had to think about once a week. My impression of Jesus was that of a one-dimensional, Sunday-morning Jesus for whom people dressed up in suits, ties, and smooth, silky robes. He wasn't someone who loved me personally and who lived in my heart and revealed Himself in my daily life.

By the time I approached high school, I had probably stopped thinking about God and the church altogether, giving my heart instead to the lesser gods of sports, girls, and athletic success. In so doing, I embarked on a long journey of living, thinking, and doing everything for one person—me. In the process, I became indoctrinated by a certain way of thinking about God, Jesus, heaven, eternity, and myself. I simply didn't give it much thought at all. I was a free spirit running wild on the earth, excelling in athletics and taking cues from the world for my youthful sense of acceptance. That was what mattered. I was learning how to succeed and perform on my own terms, and in so doing found that success was the measure of my worth.

Without knowing it, I had begun to contract a deadly disease, what I've since come to call "spiritual HIV." Like its physical counterpart, it's an aggressive, invisible disease that attacks our spiritual vitality, robbing us of sensitivity to the Holy Spirit, deadening our faith, and numbing us to the reality of the living God. And it carried me to the brink of a form of spiritual death.

# CHAPTER ONE
## Spiritual HIV

WHAT DO I MEAN BY SPIRITUAL HIV? First, let me give you some statistics that may blow your mind. They show how fast the AIDS virus spread from a relatively isolated outbreak to a global epidemic. Check this out: in the initial eight-year span in which records were kept (1981-1989), the first 100,000 cases of AIDS were reported. In the next fifteen *months*, another 100,000 cases were reported.

Statistics tell us that 31 people died of AIDS in the United States in 1981. Through the next decade, about 58,000 of those who became infected died. That's roughly the number of men and women who died in the Vietnam War. Yet in the next ten-year span, the disease exploded across the earth. From 1990 to 2000, nearly 300,000 people died from the disease.

We know the rest of the story. To date, well over a million people have died from AIDS in the U.S. alone, and that figure has grown to many millions in Africa and elsewhere.

It's shocking how fast this disease grew from a relatively obscure, confined outbreak into an unchecked global catastrophe. This disease, which destroys the human immune system, is now running rampant across the planet, decimating whole populations and, in some cultures, leaving a generation of children parentless and destitute. It is a global plague of biblical proportions.

There have been some breakthroughs, and while these haven't stopped the disease, medical science has developed potent AIDS "cocktails" that suppress, delay, and mask its most deadly symptoms. These drugs don't cure but do slow AIDS' progression, prolonging life, reducing mortality rates, and giving the appearance of allowing the afflicted to live relatively normal lives. These meds cause symptoms to lay dormant, sometimes for years, so that no one, save for someone's personal doctor, may even know they have the disease. And as we've seen with some high-profile celebrities like Magic Johnson, even though the seeds of a fatal disease course through their veins, meds such as the AZT cocktails help them to manage the disease over extended periods.

So the infected go on living, no one knows any better. Life goes on. But there's one problem—they're still sick! They're still infected with AIDS. The sick have been granted only an *illusion* of health and normalcy. And while that might give us some measure of encouragement, it's really little more than denial. It is a dangerous illusion that, probably in many cases, allows some of the afflicted to continue behaviors and attitudes that caused the infection to begin with. The disease continues to spread, and millions continue to get sick as the fallout tears at the fabric of society.

## Spiritual HIV in the Church

So what does HIV have to do with the Body of Christ? Why do I use such a drastic analogy? Because I think it describes the nature and character of a serious strain of spiritual disease running through the Church. I travel a lot, and most Christians I speak with think the Church (or at least *their* church) is doing just fine. *No problem here, thank you.* They're doing lots of nice things, have quality programs and preaching, excellent worship, a good children's ministry—the list goes on. An acquaintance recently tried to sell me on his church by describing an extensive basement remodel they'd completed, and the new couches and big-screen TV they'd given the youth ministry. Nothing wrong with fresh paint and new couches, but what is really going on in the Church of North America? What about the empowering, saving, life-changing presence of God in our midst? It pains me to say that, in my experience, that's no longer a high priority in the hierarchy of many churches' core values or pursuits. The parallels with the AIDS epidemic are unmistakable.

Traveling across the country over the past two decades, preaching to hundreds of church congregations in all parts of this country, I have observed a wide cross-section of the life that I've come to call the "Church of North America." And I have, indeed, seen and experienced any number of what I would call healthy, vital, and vibrant churches across our nation. These are invariably humble, close-knit communities of believers that have learned to focus on what is truly important and function as genuine New Testament "bodies." In these churches people are not just getting saved, being baptized, hearing good sermons, and launching new programs. They are being genuinely discipled in the Word, nurturing new believers into mature disciples and preaching to the lost. They worship with all of their hearts, wait on God, and walk in His power and anointing. The members of these fellowships are both ministering to one another and being ministered to by the power of the Holy Spirit. In the communities where these churches reside, God is being glorified in spirit and in truth. These churches move and work as living bodies of Christ and are wonderful places to behold. Honestly, though, in my experience, these churches are all too scarce.

In too many others something far different is occurring. In these can be seen patterns and practices that have left me disheartened. From coast to coast, repeated in church after church, is evidence of what I have come to identify as the Christian version of the AIDS virus. Among other things, it has resulted in the church's diminishing role in a culture that is spiraling dramatically downward.

From my vantage at the crossroads of mainstream evangelical Christianity, the plague is spreading rapidly. It is approaching epidemic proportions in the life and culture of the Church of North America. Beyond that, it underlies (and may through weakness and indifference even be partially responsible for) our culture's extraordinary moral decay. In a day when the Church has an unprecedented opportunity to impact the nation for Christ and alter the landscape for what's good and right, it has, in many cases, been transformed instead by the culture, absorbing and adopting its attitudes and behaviors. Confronted by a society racing toward the abyss of rampant secularism—a nation in feverish retreat from its biblical roots—the modern Church is a flaccid surrogate of its virile, New Testament counterpart and is becoming indistinguishable from society at large.

## Creeping Malaise

I have for the past seventeen years made my living as a traveling preacher, visiting churches, holding conferences, spiritual revivals, prayer meetings, and addressing youth groups of all persuasions, in all settings and denominations. I've seen a lot of the activity of the local church. I've gotten to know pastors and have interacted with their congregations, and I can say without a doubt that most have been almost uniformly excellent, sincere brothers and sisters in Christ. Yet what I too often encounter are frantic, frustrated, and burned-out staffs who are making herculean efforts to keep afloat dead or dying churches.

As the people of God, we are meant to be living out and expressing the abundant spiritual life afforded us by our glorious Savior. So why don't our churches reflect and embody this abundant life? How can this be, especially when these churches are busy and bustling with all manner of so-called positive activities, programs, and outreach ministries? Scratch a little deeper below the surface and you'll see the disease flourishing in its brilliant disguise. It's an infection that I've come to describe as "works without worship." These churches, filled with sincere, well-meaning Christians are, in many cases, spinning their wheels at ten thousand rpm, feverishly trying to manufacture something akin to spirituality. They're working themselves to exhaustion, getting lost in works rather than losing themselves in the One we're seeking to worship.

As I've prayed about this phenomenon and sought to understand its cause, I feel as if the Lord revealed a creeping, mostly unseen spiritual malaise at work that conspires to stifle true spirit filled ministry and to block relational intimacy. These hard-working, sincere congregations are quietly propagating the seeds of a spiritual disease that bleeds the life and vitality out of the Church. I've named this invisible sickness "spiritual HIV" because of what seems to be its viral, life-killing transmission across the Christian landscape. The virus has sapped churches both large and small, preventing the most well-meaning Christians from either experiencing or entering into a transforming relationship with Jesus Christ. From my vantage, it's spreading with a viral intensity equal to medical AIDS. Stripped of genuine New Testament community and authenticity too many of our churches have become swirling centers of perpetual motion and activity but have also, to a shocking extent, been rendered spiritually bankrupt.

## Performance-Based Acceptance

What is at the root of this spiritual HIV? What is its cause? Plainly stated, the HIV in the Christian community can be summed up in three words: *Performance Based Acceptance* (let's call it PBA). What is PBA? It is seeking to experience God's grace through human effort and good works. It is an endless striving to please Christ (and one another) through wholly external, superficial spiritual activity. It should come as no surprise that this life-killing syndrome is the natural out-growth of our type-A, appearance-based, achievement-driven culture. Unfortunately, the Church has wholly bought into it, even though the Bible repeatedly warns us against it. Our spiritual senses have grown dull, and the voices of the world shout louder and more emphatically.

The heart of PBA, at its core, lies in attempting to live the Christian life in a totally graceless manner. It forsakes the true worship that comes from a heart motivated by love for Christ alone. It places too much value on the appearance of being spiritual and bypasses genuine relationship for performance-based relationships as we deceive ourselves into believing that we're actually tasting the fullness of God's joy and peace. Let me say here that PBA is fueled by a lack of understanding about our identity in Christ. We feel like we have to perform or the acceptance will stop. So, as with the world around us, our external actions become the focus and primary motive of our Christian walk.

# CHAPTER TWO
## Spiritual Meds: The Placebo Effect

NOT UNLIKE ITS PHYSICAL COUNTERPART, the spread of spiritual HIV has triggered a proliferation of masking agents that work overtime to disguise the symptoms, yet which also prevent the immune system from violently attacking the virus. What's most surprising is that many of these "spiritual meds," as I've come to call them, have even been prescribed by our church leaders. The end result of these prescribed meds by our leaders only serve to perpetuate the disease while keeping it a secret.

Many will be very surprised to learn the source of these masking agents, which conspire to effectively lure sincere Christians into expending their spiritual lives handicapped by an undiagnosed sickness.

Many will also be shocked to learn that the so-called masking meds include some of the very tools that God has given us to grow and mature. These are tools that, with proper application, lead toward spiritual healing and wholeness. Yet because of our skewed, performance-based church culture, the very meds prescribed to heal a sick body are often administered to the patient's *harm*. These meds can distort what might produce health into another symptom in need of masking.

So, what are they?

The spiritual meds we use to hide our disease are the very things that make us feel the most spiritual: *Bible study, Bible reading, serving in the church, Scripture memorization, sharing our faith, prayer, and more Bible study.* I'll repeat: these meds that hide our sickness are, in many cases, core spiritual disciplines. Don't misunderstand: with the right emphasis, in a healthy, balanced walk, they're indeed invaluable tools. In the proper context, and with the right motives, they illuminate and bring the truth into focus. Individually and collectively, these disciplines add value, depth, and texture to our walk of faith. With correct application they stimulate growth and maturity. Each discipline, rightly understood, serves a valuable purpose, increasing our knowledge of God, instilling principles of godliness, and helping us to hear and recognize His voice.

Sounds good to me. So what could be so wrong? Quite simply, there's nothing wrong with these disciplines—in fact, far from it. Yet here's the catch: when performed as rote exercises from a sense of obligation to make us feel more spiritual or to gain acceptance within our spheres, they're little more than dry, sterile "works." In this sense, they become chores on a checklist to cross off so that we can move on with our day.

Sure, in the process, we'll discover all kinds of stuff about God and learn a host of amazing truths about faith, salvation, and walking out our Christian witness. That's obviously a good and necessary thing. But without a fully engaged heart, mind, and spirit intimately and humbly connected to the Lord of all, even these rich disciplines possess no spiritual power in themselves. They cannot, by our mere repetitive practice or well-meaning immersion, deepen our desire or produce greater godliness. They are, in this context, little more than pleasant-tasting spiritual meds mimicking true manna.

What I see modeled and practiced as New Testament spirituality in the Church of North America in the twenty-first century is this: Christians are buying into a placebo life of works without worship. They are invested in a form of legalism without lordship, and the Church has become occupied with methodical serving without seeking. All of this has manifested in a church culture that has, in many cases, come to measure itself by the intensity of its motion and uninterrupted "doing." It has produced people who are obsessed with performance and acceptance but who only mimic the *appearance* of living Spirit-filled lives.

## Works Without Worship

When I think of works without worship, I have only to go back to my seminary experience. This unfortunate pattern did not manifest as a result of poor teaching or bad theology but of my own spiritual disposition at the time. I was serving as a youth pastor, doing youth pastor stuff, running around preaching and praying and getting things done, largely on automatic pilot. Sure, I watched God work in people's lives. Good stuff, *great* stuff was happening. All the trappings were there—I looked and acted the part of a youth pastor, yet in my own heart, the deep affectionate, passionate pursuit of Christ wasn't there. I simply didn't know it at the time.

Without realizing it, I had allowed myself to slide into an easy reliance on works to carry me, to fill the void I had not yet learned to identify. I came to believe that the work itself would compensate for my gaping lack of knowing the enlivening presence of God in my life and my ministry. In the years since, I've come to realize how I substituted one for another, works for worship. Our culture does that to us. Jesus said go and tell, but He also said *come and see.* Yet the focus of evangelistic outreach frequently becomes little more than to get people to come to church.

Church in this context becomes a means to an end—an activity—a predictable event steeped in programs rather than in a Person. There's no depth of ministry or power. We work to get people to come to our church services, proudly showcasing our programs, hoping they'll come to Christ, but we've left Jesus on the sidelines. God's sweet presence is nowhere to be found. As a result, we've lost the mentality of being light and salt in the biblical sense. We're doing the right stuff without the right motive, without the right *motor*. We're doing church work without doing the work of the church.

One major aspect of our salvation is to delight ourselves in the Lord and become a people who worship Him in spirit and in truth. We are called to embark on an epic, unpredictable adventure with our Creator. Yet we focus on works to fill the void, and it only serves to spin us off track, burn us out, and dry us up.

## Legalism Without Lordship

In Galatians 4:8-10, Paul says, "Now that you know God, how is it you are turning back to weak or miserable principles?" Paul was dealing with the early Jewish believers who were still trying to make themselves good enough to gain God's favor by keeping laws and customs *(Romans 10:3-4)*. That's legalism. And as we know, that's not God's way of salvation.

Yet legalism creeps back into our church culture where we least expect it. Why? Because it cooperates so seamlessly with our instinctive human need to quantify and measure our Christianity against a list of "to do's." Check your Bible study off the list, do your good deed for the day, pray over lunch, and call it good. In many respects, we're no different from the Old Testament Jews in that we're all about results. Legalism thrives on external, outward appearances and quantifiable *results*. There's nothing wrong with results. But God help us if, in the spirit realm, we think we truly know the result of something. Much of Christianity occurs in the mysterious, unquantifiable realm. We *want* it to be predictable and paint-by-numbers, but our God is a mysterious God. We want manageability, but God desires us to wade out deeper in the murky waters of trust, and into unseen realms where little is clearly defined or understood.

If we can't abide these uncomfortable conditions, we'll sit up in the stands and cheer on those courageous few warriors doing it on the playing field for real. It's safe up in the stands. But safety leads to apathy, and apathy leads to spiritual poverty *every time*. This is one of the dangers of legalism. It's safe and routine. It robs us of the mystery and wonder of pursuing God with a childlike passion.

I recall a sad scene from my time at seminary. I'm sitting on the couch, nestled comfortably in my quiet little cocoon, reading the Word, enjoying my precious quiet time. My wife Laura walks in the room and innocently asks me a question. Without even looking up, I barked back, *"Can't you see I'm having my quiet time?"* Whoa, man! I've used my precious quiet time as an excuse to scorch my wife with my tongue. Is that sick or what? If that doesn't speak for itself about my heart, and the rigid, arid spirit of duty I labored under, I don't know what could. I brought my checklist mode of spirituality into what should've been the sweetest and most transforming of spiritual pleasures. I had been ingesting a spiritual med that hid my true condition. I had my quiet time, so I'm good to go. Just don't interrupt me.

Are we meeting Jesus in our disciplines? Are we seeking and seeing His face? Are we delighting ourselves in His presence and resting in His Word? Or are we, in our chronic spiritual anemia, turning quiet times and Bible studies into spiritual multi-vitamins. I popped a dose of daily quiet time today. That'll last me until tomorrow. I'm a good Christian compared to all those guys I know who didn't have their quiet time. But a multi-vitamin is no defense against HIV. We've substituted morality and goodness and the appearance of spirituality for a passionate love affair with Christ. It's an empty proposition. This trade-off has left us bankrupt and the Church in crisis. I'll even step out and suggest that God could care less about us being "good" Christians. He wants us to be in love with Him.

### Serving Without Seeking
People love to serve. That's a good thing, an awesome thing. People in the institutional Church of North America are, by and large, excellent servers. But, once again, what is our motive? Are we serving out of a vibrant heart of Spirit-led joy or has serving become another

form of a masking med disguising our infirmity? Case in point: I have a good friend whose wife not long ago underwent emergency surgery after experiencing a sudden illness. This woman happened to be a relatively young mom of four children and, while the surgery went well, the entire family braced themselves for what would be a difficult, months-long recovery. In no time a list of volunteers had lined up to provide meals, mow lawns, run errands, babysit, give rides, and a host of other helpful tasks. The meals started coming and coming, and they kept coming. This family was blessed beyond words to find that they did not have to make a meal for nearly two months.

It was by any measure a tremendous outpouring of Christian service addressing, in the most practical way, an urgent felt need in the Body. But that isn't the whole story. What is equally telling is that, as grateful as the family was and forever will be for those meals and errands, they recalled later with some dismay that, of the dozens of Christians who showed up with steaming, delicious pots and baskets full of food, few stopped long enough to actually *pray*. These generous meal-providers apparently felt no impulse (or possibly no confidence) to share anything but the most punctuated greetings—no meaningful verse from the Bible, no one willing (or bold enough) to lay hands on and pray for continued healing. Few took the time to sit down to listen and empathize about ongoing fears or the emotional trauma of the surgery. Now, don't get me wrong, many of these folks certainly didn't want to intrude or make a fuss. Most were simply uncomfortable delving deeper. But isn't this the Church of Jesus Christ we're talking about? We were saved in order to minister not just to a lost and dying world but to one another.

Those Christians were there to serve, and serve they did, excellently. But in the dozens of face-to-face encounters with a family wrestling to recover from the aftershocks of a serious illness, effectively no genuine ministry occurred. What are the odds? How many Christians are left to fend for their own spiritual well-being by a Church that goes the extra mile to keep a safe distance, is strictly hands off and uneasy about going deeper, and justifies it all because plenty of "stuff" is getting done?

## Performance Without Power

Finally, Christians have bought into a religious formula best described by the phrase *performance without power.*

Isn't this precisely what the Bible categorically warns us against— performing for God and our brothers and sisters? Like the world, we attempt to please God through works when what God truly desires is our hearts. Summed up, this is the heart of PBA: seeking to please God through external spiritual activity and pursuing a sense of righteousness through our obedience to a set of rules.

When I was a little kid, my parents bought me a rocking horse. I'd get my cowboy hat on and ride that thing like John Wayne.

There was a lot of motion, a lot of energy expended, but it didn't get me anywhere. Too much of what we do in the church is like that rocking horse. We move around and exhaust ourselves, relying on our programmatic activity to create the veneer of busyness when we should be investing that time waiting on, praying to, and, with passionate intensity, pursuing Him. Instead, we're often content to keep rocking back and forth but getting nowhere.

This is why the deep spiritual "God stuff" that we really need and crave and really want to see happening is not happening. We've grown accustomed to being satisfied with the "appearance" of something happening, but there really is very little anointed ministry going on in most churches today. What's so tragic is that I truly believe there's a remnant who discern the problem and who truly desire more—sincere believers who desperately desire to taste and experience authentic New Testament Christianity. But where can they go? All they know is what's been presented to them. They don't know anything different.

The root of performance-based Christianity arises from our need to be accepted and from serving out of a sense of obligation. This is radically distinct and diametrically opposed to the experience of power and blessing flowing from a living romance with the Lover of our Souls. Rather than being enlivened by the Holy Spirit, PBA is letting external activities serve as the substitute for an inner witness, replacing a true love and desire for God.

How is it that we have bought into our nation's culture of obligatory service and become satisfied with the *appearance* of being spiritual? How is it that God's people have twisted the rich heritage of spiritual disciplines into a means of pleasing ourselves and impressing others? Like Esau, we've sold our birthright for a pot of porridge, whereas, in truth, we would be well advised to pour ourselves out, provoking one another into a passionate quest for Christ. We've become fat and satisfied comparing our lukewarm faith with the ice-cold temperature of our peers and, somehow, feeling good about it all. Rather than seeking and serving the One to whom we're eternally indebted, the One through whom and from whom all blessings flow, we've taken to catering to the fickle tastes of those whose acceptance we're really seeking.

Don't misunderstand. I wonder if we've all been deceived to an extent into taking our spiritual meds like good, albeit chronically ill patients, exchanging a vibrant, red-hot romance with the living Christ for good deeds and dutiful Bible reading.

In a day when the Church desperately needs to be carving deep inroads into the post-Christian culture, preaching, loving, and ministering with courage and boldness borne of a dynamic intimacy with the living Vine, our PBA checklist approach is surrendering territory on all fronts. And it is sowing seeds of outward emptiness for generations to come.

Here's what I haven't shared with you, and it's what makes me such an expert on this topic: I have for much of my life been the chief practitioner of performance-based Christianity. My youth and young Christian adulthood were steeped in a performance-based mindset. I grew up in a performance-based culture and learned to perform and excel by *those* rules in *that* world. Growing up as a young man playing sports, I sought the glory that came with exceptional performance. I carried the heavy baggage of that works-driven mindset into full-time ministry.

It's a story I'm sure many of you will relate to.

# CHAPTER THREE

## My Four-Headed God

AT ITS SPIRITUAL ROOT, there is nothing uglier than the heart of performance-based acceptance (PBA). Yet it was this mindset that infected me at a young age and propelled me into adulthood. Worse, it came to define my early Christian ministry experience as well. Allow me to clarify: there's nothing fundamentally wrong with the basic human desire of wanting to be accepted. We all share a deep desire to be loved, admired, and accepted for who we are regardless of our flaws.

It is a core need of ours, in fact, that springs from an innate, God-given desire. Every person has a deep thirst in their soul for being loved and accepted; God gives us this desire. This longing to be loved and accepted grows from the God-sized hole that exists in every human spirit. Yet, growing up in, and daily conditioned by, our man-centered culture, the driving focus of our inherent longing can become twisted and corrupted. While we long to be accepted for who we are, in this carnal world we quickly learn to derive our sense of acceptance and approval not from who we are but from what we *do*—and this not from God but from mankind.

Alienated from God and pressing our own agenda, closed off to His love and, more than likely, weighed down in our sin, we invariably end up seeking all manner of lesser things to fill that hole. In my case, this seeking after lesser things—sports and athletic success—became a powerful addiction early in life. And, honestly, at the time, there seemed to be no greater goal I could either desire or achieve than to excel as an athlete.

All I have to do is look back to my childhood, growing up in Huntsville, to identify the root. From an early age, sports filled my world. My dad was my coach—and he was great at it. Looking back at those days, as a father myself, I can truly appreciate his heart and see the sacrifices he made, carving time away from a busy career as a NASA engineer to coach his sons. He had to teach himself the fundamentals of coaching baseball and football, and then, by pouring through sports manuals and rule books, he guided my brother and I through some exciting years in the Huntsville youth leagues.

My first taste of athletics was in fifth grade, playing "115-pound" football at the YMCA. I was younger than most of the guys on the field and still had baby fat, but because of my age, I was allowed to weigh a little more than the limit. That first year I played offensive and defensive tackle—not exactly glory positions, but it was a good intro to the rough-and-tumble of the game.

The next year, my dad started coaching and switched me to quarterback. Suddenly, at a young age, I was the big dog playing the glamour position of quarterback. I had found my true athletic calling.

I quickly began to excel and taste a kind of success—and, yes, acceptance—that would forge my identity for years to come. Because of my dad's skill as a coach and the special group of athletes on our team, we hardly ever lost in those early years—even playing against older, more physically mature teams. I later learned that dad scheduled games against older teams to toughen us up.

So it was on the athletic field, during this initial phase of my early sports experience, that I first tasted that heady buzz of performance-based acceptance. As I achieved more and more success playing quarterback on some truly great Little League teams, my desire for more success, more recognition, more backslaps and special treatment only intensified. This mentality that I eagerly adopted is a seductive drug, commonly drilled into the hearts of young men and women during their most formative years. It lies at the core of our society and even the Body of Christ. The lesson it teaches is potent and long-lasting: we value people based on what they do, not on who they are. Christian or not, the message follows us into adulthood: credentials matter more than character.

When we bring this attitude into our relationship with Jesus and His people, it can become a deadly disease. Though ours was a church-going family, by this stage of my life, caught up as I was in the flurry and excitement of worldly reward and approval, church lost all relevance for me. Without really being aware it was happening, I had fallen prey to a dominating, "jock-centric" worldview.

Beyond junior high school, the spiritual side of my life faded altogether as athletics became my sole source of significance and focus. I call it my four-headed god—*football, basketball, baseball, and track.* By my freshman year of high school, I had begun to experience even more success on the football field. I was a multi-sport athlete but had dropped baseball altogether by then to pursue our football team's goal of completing an undefeated season. And, in fact, the ninth grade team I quarterbacked ended the season as one of the few teams in Alabama history to finish undefeated, untied, and un-scored upon.

Most teams didn't cross the 50-yard line against our defense. "City Champs!" read the headlines. Need I say it: this performance and reward stuff tasted pretty sweet to my ninth grade ego. The next year, I played varsity as a sophomore, something that almost never happened at our school. And by my junior and senior year, I was starting on a powerhouse Alabama high school football team, first as a running back and, by my senior year, as starting quarterback.

At the start of my senior year, it wasn't uncommon to have a number of Division 1 scouts attending our practices. Talk about feeding your ego! I had learned the recipe for success in high school football—hard work equals excellent performance equals over-the-top performance-based-approval ratings—and I was working it overtime. God had given me raw athletic talent, and by the start of my senior year, I'd become the second most sought after football recruit in Alabama and one of the top 100 recruits in the country. Here I was, a high school All-American quarterback and All-Region basketball player, ready to sign a letter of intent to play football for any college in the country I wanted—Florida, LSU, Georgia Tech, Auburn. It doesn't take a genius to understand that all of this added up to one, single, obsessive focus—ME! I love this PBA!

It's not hard to visualize all of the ways in which this performance-based approval can corrupt a soul. Yes, I had been raised in the church. But in the face of this kind of early adulation, why would I need God? I was worshipping richly and deeply at the altar of self-indulgence. Truth be told, I had eagerly adjusted to the life, as it were, of a high school rock star. Very few things an average, hormone-driven teenage boy could possibly desire escaped my grasp. The corruption of my soul was advancing at breakneck speed.

Exploiting the notoriety my athletic achievements had earned, I became a user of things and people. Little did I know that my life was about to be changed forever. During this whirlwind of my senior year, I was asked to play in Alabama's North-South All-Star game, and was selected as captain for the North team. As I traveled to Tuscaloosa for the beginning of the All-Star week of practices, I didn't know that God had the coming week marked on His calendar as well.

# CHAPTER FOUR
## Save Me, Jesus

I CAN REMEMBER IT LIKE IT WAS LAST WEEK. In a hot, sweaty little room on the campus of the University of Alabama, one of the coaches of our North Alabama All-Star football team stood sharing his testimony. The tale he told was eerily similar to the one I'd been living for the past four years—a sordid legacy of athletic success, fleshly sin, and self-absorption. Suddenly, I felt my face start to flush and my heart begin to race, and a deep sense of nervous shame inexplicably began to wash over me. I glanced at the guy next to me, a short, stocky linebacker named John Knox who went on to play at the University of Alabama. Out of the corner of my eye, I noticed that he was weeping, holding his face in his hands. Then, I swear I could hear a deep, agonizing groan coming from the depths of his gut.

It was the night before the All-Star game, the end of a week of hot, humid, intense, three-a-day practices. The coaches invited us all to come to a voluntary meeting, for what purpose we didn't know. I had just wandered in after dinner with a bunch of players from all over the state when one of the coaches marched up to the microphone and started sharing. As we sat listening, unsure of what was coming, the coach began giving his testimony about how Jesus Christ had saved him from a life of sin and sex and *ego*. I thought we were going to talk about the next night's game or discuss strategy, but *whoa*, that got my attention. Here was a successful former player and coach telling our story, reading our mail, addressing some of the nation's best high school football players on a level that most of us had not experienced.

It was July 29, 1976, and I had been tabbed to be the starting quarterback for the North squad. I'd arrived in Tuscaloosa riding a wave of glory and basking in self-satisfaction. I'd been named MVP of the City of Huntsville and, soon after, showed up near the top of a list of the top 100 football recruits in the nation.

I'd already signed a letter of intent to play at Auburn University, about four hours from Huntsville on the southeastern plains of Alabama. While I could've signed with a number of top Division 1 football programs, including perennial powerhouse Alabama, Auburn's first-year coach, Doug Barfield, simply out-recruited everyone else to get me. And he recruited me to play *quarterback*! I was his first recruit, a detail he reminded me about many years later when he showed up unexpectedly at my induction into the Huntsville-Madison County Sports Hall of Fame.

Leading up to the game, I'd been training like a maniac all summer, preparing myself for college, but also to fulfill my high school goal of not just playing in the state All-Star game, but starring in it. And now, sitting in this little room, squirming in my seat as this humble coach stood sharing his life, it all kind of melted away. I felt as if I heard God speaking directly to me, almost audibly asking me, *Foster, what have you done with your own life, with all of the gifts I've given you?*

In my mind, a slow-motion highlight reel of my athletic exploits began to rewind. I began mentally reciting back to the Lord all of my various accomplishments and awards, thinking perhaps to justify myself yet feeling a growing unease in the depths of my soul, somehow profoundly aware that all of it, in fact, amounted to *less than nothing.*

As the speaker continued and the Holy Spirit began landing on other players, many began to cover their faces and weep. It was in that electric moment that I realized, for the first time in my life, that I was a sinner. I do not exaggerate when I say it was devastating. Coming face-to-face with the reality of my sin was easily the most physically empty feeling I've ever felt before or since. It was my Isaiah 6 moment, a flash of self-revelation in which I spiritually curled up in a fetal position and screamed in my heart, *Woe is me! I am ruined!*

One of the coaches gave an invitation for the players to respond and give their lives to Christ. Tears were now streaming down my face, and when he asked us to pray with him, my head dropped into my hands and I told Jesus, "I'm a sinner. I need You to save me."

It was nothing complicated. It was a simple prayer: *I am a sinner. I need a Savior. Save me, Jesus. Change my life forever.*

When I said *Amen*, a physical sensation I can only describe as profound peace and restfulness washed over me. It was as if I'd pulled up my spiritual lawn chair under a palm tree on a white sand beach and felt instant release. The feeling was profound freedom from a relentless, performance-based lifestyle that had dominated me since childhood.

To be honest, it was the first time I'd even thought about God since I was a freshman in high school, attending church and going through those same old motions. And then suddenly God lands on me in this totally impromptu setting, during what I figured to be the biggest week of my athletic career to date, and I had no idea what hit me. I walked back to the dorm dazed and abuzz with a certainty that something radical and inexplicable had happened to me. I knew I'd been changed and, in some way, had touched eternity. But I quickly returned to the here and now, remembered I had a game to play and an MVP award to win. So I purposed in my mind to set it all aside until later.

The game, for me, was disappointing and anticlimactic. Frankly, it was the worst game of my high school career. And it began with the first snap of the ball—a wretched fumble. From that moment on, the starting center and I couldn't get in sync all night long, and we kept fumbling. And when we didn't fumble, I was running for my life on almost every pass play. Our offensive line could not protect me, and I had no time all night long to do anything, as what turned out to be a dominating opposing defense just swarmed in at will.

Late in the second half, I was sitting on the bench, all hope of winning MVP of the All-Star game gone in a blaze of sacks and turnovers. I sat there steeped in self-pity, thinking it wasn't supposed to happen this way. I had prepared my whole life for this game, and to have the worst game of my career simply didn't compute. To add insult to injury, the head coach for Auburn, the team that had just signed this All-American to play for them, was sitting in the stands. I was truly humiliated.

The tight end on our team was a guy named Tim Travis, a strong Christian who had been talking to me about Jesus all week long. He saw me sitting miserably on the bench and tried to encourage me, but I was inconsolable. I turned it over in my mind and thought maybe, now that I'm a Christian, this very public failure was a cosmic pay-back of sorts. I assumed I had some serious penance to pay for the hellacious life I'd lived and, in that mortifying moment, it seemed as if a big combat boot in the sky had punted me through the uprights. It was a hard way to end my high school career, but in hindsight, I can see that it had a huge impact on my spiritual life heading into college. God slowly began to change my priorities. He didn't change my intensity, because I would soon become just as intense about Christ as I had been about sports. Not surprisingly, I'd soon seamlessly transfer my performance-based acceptance personality to my immature faith. As for football, God began to loosen its strangle hold on a high school All-American from Huntsville.

Sitting glumly on the bench in what was to have been the biggest game of my career, ready to leave for Auburn's summer camp in a few weeks, my lifelong obsession was already starting to evaporate. Unfortunately, the seeds of spiritual HIV had been planted in my character and had sunk their roots deep.

# CHAPTER FIVE

# A New Heart, Old Patterns

IN THE WEEKS LEADING UP to my time at Auburn, fresh off the All-Star Game disappointment, there was no mistaking that God had given me a new heart. The problem is He didn't erase my memory banks. Enjoying my first taste of major college football with the new surroundings, new teammates, and unfamiliar routine of college life, I loved the Lord and read my Bible but my mind remained a battlefield. At night, the moment my head hit the pillow after classes and practice, that movie reel began to roll, replaying the highlights and lowlights of an Alabama high school quarterback. While I absolutely felt like a new creature in Christ, some of the old patterns of selfishness, ego, and pride persisted.

From the beginning of my time at Auburn, I attended strong churches, strong at least in what I understood at the time to be genuine discipleship. But even then, just as in athletics, I found myself primarily focused on the constant act of doing and not being. As a young Christian, I didn't know the difference, but looking back, the focus of my church activity in those days seemed to be on gaining knowledge and expending effort rather than on internal change or the condition of my heart.

In 1 Samuel 16:7, God tells the prophet, "Man looks at the outward appearance, but the Lord looks at the heart." God wanted my heart, but the emphasis of my church involvement in those days was a well-intentioned focus on spiritual disciplines more than on Jesus. The programs in these churches were challenging and accomplished good things; they seemed to be Christ-driven. In hindsight, I trained most of my focus on all of the good programs, Bible studies, and small groups as opposed to my individual pursuit of Christ. The programs propped me up as a believer rather than lead me deeper. Don't get me wrong, it was all good stuff, part of the natural "discipleship" of a young believer you'll find at most churches. But perhaps it was also an early sign of a flawed emphasis within my church walk, and in the church itself, because while it kept me busy it didn't lead me into true intimacy. Quite the contrary, it actually perpetuated my PBA inclinations. My early impressions were that Church was a "buffet" of sorts from which to pick and choose what I wanted to do.

At the same time, my football career at Auburn wasn't panning out as I'd expected. Early in my freshman year, our starting fullback went down with an injury, leaving a big hole in the backfield. I wasn't getting many reps at quarterback and, hungry to compete, I quickly informed the coach that I thought I could help the team at fullback.

They gave me a look, and I quickly worked my way up to become the starter, remaining at fullback most of my college career. My sophomore year I won the best blocker award in spring practice, but by my junior year, I'd been switched to tight end and my role on the team was becoming increasingly unclear.

Truth be told, I'd been losing my zeal for football for a long time. The politics of the college game wore me down. Meanwhile, I'd become highly active in the Fellowship of Christian Athletes at Auburn and started traveling around the state, giving my testimony to youth groups and churches. These folks loved Auburn football and Auburn football players. I loved the eager reception I always received and relished the chance to share my faith.

During college I interned at Whitesberg Baptist Church in Huntsville and went on my first mission trip. I drove with 26 other guys in a bus to Philadelphia, and the first guy I shared Christ with—a big burly cop standing on the street corner—got saved. I walked straight up to him and started sharing my testimony. Tears started flowing down his face. He took his hat off, leaned up against the wall, and said, "This is what I've needed all my life."

Later, as we sang songs about Jesus on the portable bleachers at JFK Plaza with our little sound system, up walks this big dude with two Dobermans. He was wearing a dress, high heels, and a wig. Gangs were selling drugs on the street corners, we were surrounded by the colorful citizens of Philadelphia's toughest neighborhood, and in that moment, facing this giant transvestite, I realized that ministry can be as wild and crazy as running head-on into a linebacker.

I also learned on that trip that I had successfully transferred my competitive drive in football directly into performing for the Lord. One guy on the trip was gifted in personal evangelism, reeling in the lost left and right like a champion bass fisherman. My reaction? I'm almost ashamed to say that rather than praising God for the new believers, it got my competitive juices flowing. All I could think was, *Man, I've got to get on the stick and save me a few people.*

What a shocker, huh? Performance-based-acceptance meets ambitious street evangelist.

By fall of my senior year, I have to say, I was ready for football to be over. I remember walking off the field after our last game with Mike McQuaig, one of my closest friends on the planet. We had just lost to the University of Alabama for the fourth time in four years. We looked into each other's eyes, bittersweet smiles on our faces, and both said, simultaneously, "It's over." And I'm not kidding; the feeling was simply indescribable relief. I'd excelled as a starting fullback in college. I'd made it through four years without a serious injury or major surgery. While I broke my right hand three times, tore ligaments in my left thumb, and dislocated my left shoulder, I walked off the field that final time without a limp and (this is no small thing) I didn't have chronic headaches or memory loss.

I felt truly fortunate. My education had been paid for. And now it was over. I was satisfied and ready to start a new life. I had great hopes and lofty ideals, but a long journey lay before me.

## U-Turn Into Ministry

As an education major with an emphasis in marketing, I took a job after graduation as a regional sales manager at Warren-Sherer, a commercial refrigeration company just outside of Atlanta. Warren-Sherer builds the refrigerated display showcases you see in supermarkets. My wife Laura and I moved to my new territory near Orlando, Florida, and we lived in a 1,000-square-foot starter home near Disney World. We were ready to grab our little slice of the American dream.

By my fifth year, I was making good money, we belonged to a good church, and I was working with the youth group. Yet as the job became more lucrative, my satisfaction plunged.

I was teaching 12th grade Sunday school, and the pastors knew I had been praying about some serious life changes. Then, in March 1987, a guest preacher spoke at our church, saying, "If God is leading you to do something, you need to be urgent about it." For the past several months, I had been feeling a strong pull toward vocational ministry, but that day I knew. The youth pastor saw me coming toward the front during a ministry response time, took my hand, and said, "I know what's going on, but I want to hear you say it." I took a deep breath and prayed, *God, if this is You calling me into vocational ministry, then I'm trusting You to do it.*

The pastors had been strongly encouraging me to go to seminary, and Laura and I decided upon New Orleans Baptist Theological Seminary. I decided I'd tell my boss at a big sales conference in Chicago. I walked straight up to the VP of Regional Sales, a fine Christian man, and it was almost like he already knew.

"Foster," he said, "I'm happy for you, son."

I resigned shortly afterwards, filled with the same sense of relief I'd felt after my last Auburn football game. Laura and I began to prepare to move our little family to New Orleans for this next uncertain season of life. In many respects, it felt like we were walking into the Twilight Zone, and that wasn't far off the mark. The journey would take us to New Orleans and a seminary experience that would usher in a season of brokenness I could never have imagined. Had I known then what I was walking into, I might have turned and run as fast as I could.

# CHAPTER SIX
## The "C-Word"

IT WAS DECEMBER 13, 1988, a day that will forever thunder in my soul. I was sitting in my urologist's office after an extremely unpleasant examination. Dr. Schwartz was staring intently at my chart, rubbing his brow.

"That's a malignant tumor," he said matter-of-factly, "and we need to get it out of there."

My mouth dropped open. A warm, tingling sensation washed over my body and I could feel my heart thump violently against my ribcage. The only thing I could say was, "*When?*"

"How about tomorrow?" he asked, his tone telling me it wasn't a suggestion.

I stared at the floor and nodded mutely. Then I signed some paperwork and agreed to show up early the next morning for surgery. I walked to my car in a sort of trance, thinking—*hoping*—it was a dream and begging God under my breath to wake me up. I didn't wake up. It was real. And more than at any time before or since, I was terrified.

I was in my second year of seminary at New Orleans Baptist Theological Seminary, training for student ministry and serving as a youth pastor at the First Baptist Church of New Orleans. It had been a tough, rigorous year-and-a-half of school and studying, but I was excited at what God was doing in my life. And now *this*. With no warning, everything secure and familiar in my little world had been turned upside down. Before I'd even had a chance to pray or talk to my wife, my mind was overwhelmed and totally consumed with the "C-word." Something that only happened to other people had now happened to me, and I didn't know how to deal with it.

When I walked in the door of our tiny seminary apartment, Laura asked, "How did the appointment go?"

I swallowed hard and said, "The doctor told me I have cancer." She laughed and said, "Stop it. What did he *really* say?"

Then she saw the dazed look in my eyes. She knew. We held each other for a long time, crying and praying and asking God for mercy. The next morning, still in a stupor, I went in and had the cancerous tumor removed. After I woke up and the grogginess began to fade, I could feel the fear welling up again stronger than before, wondering if Dr. Schwartz had gotten it all. I dreaded the prospect of a months-long process of chemotherapy and imagined I might be sick, in one form or another, for an extended period of time. A once proud, fearless athlete was now facing his mortality and was scared. It was like facing fourth and long against the Crimson Tide with no play to turn to.

The next time I sat down again with Dr. Schwartz, he gave me two options: constant monitoring with CAT scans and blood work or radical surgery. And not just any surgery. The procedure would cut me from naval to sternum, clean me out, scrape deep tissues and remove my lymph glands to make sure the cancer was gone. The chances for major complications were great, and these grim options made me start to come unglued. And yet I could sense the Lord stirring me, trying to tell me something.

While I wasn't yet a tested and mature Christian, I knew God was trying to get my attention. And looking back, something like spiritual scales fell from my eyes, revealing the true state of my spiritual condition. My cancer diagnosis and recovery were the beginning steps in my spiritual recovery, the first baby steps, it turned out, toward genuine spiritual maturity.

The urologist's diagnosis that morning was a physical portrait of the terminal spiritual condition of my soul. My performance-based personality had metastasized into a bona fide spiritual cancer that translated directly into my approach to God. In the process, my heart had become choked off to the flow of God's Spirit in my life. I had turned good spiritual disciplines into tried and true Christian rituals—early morning devotions, Bible reading, prayer, church service, sharing my faith; *check, check, check*—and along the way transforming myself into a paint-by-numbers Pharisee.

In the days following my surgery, I periodically lapsed into depression and my faith faltered mightily, so certain was I that I would die and leave my wife and little daughter, two-year-old Ann-Marie, alone. I opted out of final exams at seminary, knowing that within the week I would have to make a decision on whether to let them split me from crotch to clavicle like a frog on a spit. I pled with God. *What do I do?* I heard nothing but deafening silence. I asked again and again, *God... what... do... I... do?*

Awful, piercing silence was all I heard in reply.

Where had I gone wrong? What had I missed along the way? Slowly, God began to retrace my path for me, playing back my seasons of life, prompting memories of seemingly trivial moments. He called to mind scriptures that spoke to a legalistic life pattern, like Proverbs 27:19, "As water reflects a face, so a man's heart reflects the man." My heart was reflecting the wrong Jesus.

In a succession of early mornings when I was unable to sleep, God revealed to me ugliness and self-absorption. Here I was in seminary, serving in the church, supposedly living for God. What was I doing? What was I thinking? I had pastored a youth group that finished in the top 20 for baptisms in the state of Louisiana. By appearances, I was succeeding. Life was rich. It all looked good from the outside. But I was painting by the numbers, living for *man's* approval, succeeding once again according to a worldly standard.

Lord have mercy.

# CHAPTER SEVEN
## I Want Your Heart

THERE ARE DEFINING MOMENTS in a Christian's walk when God's presence manifests itself in a totally new and startling way. He touches our lives and circumstances in ways we're not accustomed in order to snap us to attention, change our hearts, or perhaps reveal wrong attitudes. Mostly, these tend to be subtle and discreet, arising in quiet moments. They're less a mighty thunderclap than a gentle whisper nudging us to attention.

And then there are the times when God shows up in such a dramatic way that everything changes, bringing new insights and shattering every illusion we hold dear. For better or worse, encounters like this typically reveal fractures in our relationship with God and our identity in His Son.

While most chapters of the Bible relate God's invasion into man's temporal space in one form or another, I'd guess that for most Christians these moments are extremely rare, arriving unexpectedly or perhaps in response to a desperate cry for deliverance.

This latter example is how God revealed Himself to me in the days following my cancer surgery. As I've shared, these were days of deep despair, worry, and gloom. My choices seemed grim: lifelong monitoring or radical, invasive surgery. Doubting my own survival, I entered a feverish season of anxiety. Life as I knew it was coming to an end.

Captive to these hallucinatory thoughts, I went to bed on a bitter cold December night in 1988, having decided to undergo radical surgery. I had finally surrendered to the awful inevitability of it and agreed to submit myself again to the scalpel, facing surgery that would leave lasting scars and, more than likely, some level of physical incapacity.

As Laura lay peacefully beside me, I tossed and turned through the night, trying to sleep. Through hours of fitful prayer and complaining to God, I heaped guilty curses upon myself for sins both real and imagined.

*Why me, God? Why are you doing this to me? What did I do to deserve this?*

When bad things happen, we tend to look inside and often blame ourselves. So certain was I that God was disciplining me for some character flaw or perceived infraction, I believe that if you had put Job and I in the same room, Job would have run away, with his hands cupped over his ears from my whining.

Suddenly, I was wide awake. I recall an almost audible voice whispering, *Get your Bible and go out to the couch.* I lay there for another few minutes before I realized it was the Holy Spirit trying to get my attention. *Get Up! Go out on the couch. It's time for us to have a heart-to-heart conversation.*

Dragging myself out of bed and into the front room with my Bible, I turned on the light and sat down, immediately sensing in my heart a verse from Hebrews: "My son, do not make light of the Lord's discipline, and do not lose heart when He rebukes you, because the Lord disciplines those He loves, and He punishes everyone He accepts as a son" *(Hebrews 12:5-8).*

The Scripture confirmed what I had long suspected. God was in fact disciplining me. It pained my heart because, as every child knows, discipline seems pretty harsh at the moment. Yet in that moment, sitting on the couch in our little studio apartment, God began speaking to the deep, hidden issues of my life, tying everything back to my performance-based spiritual circuitry.

In those next minutes, I lost all track of time, and everything flooded back—the athletics, the coaching, and the high flush of ego and acceptance that came from being a top 100 All-American college recruit. And then He began walking me back through the steps of my journey toward legalism: the spiritual checklist, the programs and processes and rote devotional times, the performance-based service, all associated with my PBA perception of Christian success. And then the darker seasons of youthful hedonism, lust, the fleshly tendencies from my past, never dealt with.

And then the familiar whisper: *Foster, I'm pruning you, but… you're not going to die.*

A warm sensation filled my body. Unlike anything I'd ever known, in that moment I understood God's sweet, intimate presence assuring me: *Foster, I want your heart. I don't care about your performance. I want your heart… and I want it in the secret places.*

I sat there, tears welling my eyes, asking, "God…what do I do?"

Again, but this time in a loud voice, I heard: *You don't need to do anything. You're healed.*

I had never known God to speak to me like that before and nearly jumped off the couch. I heard myself asking loudly, "*What?*" fearing I'd wake Laura.

*You're healed!*

From there He took me to Hosea 6:1: "Come, let us return to the Lord. He has torn us to pieces but He will heal us; He has injured us but He will bind up our wounds." I'd read this verse dozens of times, but it was like I was seeing it again for the first time. This was a picture of God's grace, His unmerited favor bestowed on me in the face of intense trial. But this grace was raw and gritty, not like the grace they taught me about in Sunday school. This grace was dripping with my own blood.

In the days that followed, He began to guide me into the deeper waters of trust. In those days, the Holy Spirit woke me repeatedly in the middle of the night and directed me to get on my knees and pray. Once I spent literally hours on the cold kitchen floor, next to the door in the dead of winter. Yet I never felt the cold. It was as if I were floating in a holy bubble, basking in God's sweetness, bathing in the healing release of God's love and affirmation. I'll never forget it. It remains the defining moment of my emerging identity as both a man and a Christian.

I recall reading an old Puritan devotion that said, "The deeper the wells the brighter thy stars shine." In those intimate hours on my knees, God communicated to me the most tender love song I had ever heard, and He did it at the very lowest point of my life. The Lord landed on me, unprompted and uninvited, and through no particular worthiness of my own. I had been trying to impress God with my performance, and He wanted to simply share His love. For the first time in my Christian walk, I saw that it wasn't about what I could do for Him or how I could serve Him or how good or holy or righteous I was. He simply wanted *me*. He wanted my love, my heart and my intimate fellowship, period! "For I desire mercy, not sacrifice, and acknowledgment of God rather than burnt offerings *(Hosea 6:6)*. It rocked my world, because my ugly, sinning heart was the *last* thing I thought God wanted.

He was showing me the true definition of grace, and it was there in spite of the gristle, blood, and sinew of my raw, sinful condition. When He spoke those words, "*You're healed*," it was like a thousand-pound bomb detonating in my soul, a feeling not unlike being saved again. What followed was a sense of release and freedom, like a lion being let out of a cage. At the same time, surrounded by God's healing favor, I suffered what I'd call an Isaiah moment—"*Woe is me!*" It was a burning bush experience, a two-fold encounter. I had climbed Mount Sinai by His Spirit and in His mercy, yet it left me trembling before an awesome God. Nothing had ever been so beautiful or terrifying.

Emerging from that reverie, my worry, guilt, and doubt vanished. I knew His good pleasure, and I was instantaneously freed from performing, no strings attached. The instant God spoke it, I was indeed physically healed of cancer. The next morning, I called and cancelled the surgery.

It marked the beginning of a profound spiritual healing that would lead me into my calling in ministry and ultimately unshackle me from a far more serious spiritual form of HIV that I hadn't even identified yet. This Spirit-filled, God-anointed breakthrough served as a baby step away from my performance-based slavery.

## "Jesus-plus" Theology

Over the next days and weeks, God would gently wake me up in the middle of the night, call me out of bed and into the front room, where I would worship Him. In the past, my times with God had always amounted to a dutiful exercise of spiritual disciplines, *doing* stuff, reading, asking for things, motivated by a sense of legalistic obligation. I had been living in a Jesus-plus theological system—Jesus plus sharing my faith; Jesus plus Bible study; Jesus plus spiritual discipline. My focus was on the disciplines and not just Jesus.

God began speaking directly to my heart, asking, *Foster, can you just love Me for Me?* I began for the first time to appreciate simply *being still.* I began to learn just to listen. I began to learn about God's grace, about Him giving me what I don't deserve. And it slowly began to free me from a lifelong feeling of having to perform, even in my prayers, saying certain things in just the right way and with just the right balance of emotion and urgency in order to accomplish a task or get something in return.

Oswald Chambers told the honest-to-God truth when he wrote that the purpose for prayer is to get to know God. Yet I'd gotten so wrapped up in the church and its programs and activities and scripted sermons and processes that I had missed the Person of Jesus. And when we miss Jesus, personally, Christianity becomes a rote, lifeless drill. Rather than a Spirit-filled, living, dynamic faith, our salvation amounts to something akin to a "cross-plus theology."

It took me about a year to work it all out in my heart and in my mind. I cancelled the surgery yet went back to the doctor's office for about a year for blood work and CAT scans. The reality of what I'd heard and experienced hadn't completely taken root yet. If I felt a pain or a spasm, I'd lapse right back into, *Oh no, the cancer is back,* and the black cloud would descend. I recall a time laying in bed with Laura a couple of months after my healing, and the fear swelled to such a level that I started to panic. I began shivering and shaking. Immediately, Laura started singing and praying and—*Boom!*—the Lord unloaded a dump truck of peace on me. The presence of God flooded in.

In time I simply quit going to the doctors. My faith had reached a place where I could say to God, "I know that what You told me is true," and mean it. Dr. Schwartz wasn't convinced. As he drew blood through a needle to test for traces of cancer, I looked him square in the eye and said, "Dr. Schwarz, I want you to know there's no more cancer in my body. I'm healed."

He removed the needle and, without making eye contact, said simply, "That's good. I'm glad." I still call his office almost every year at Christmas and tell them, "I'm still cancer-free."

The first time I went back to church, the newfound presence of God in my life was so strong that all I could do was weep during worship. My heart was so raw, like it had a giant turf burn on it. Once we started singing hymns, His love so overwhelmed me that I couldn't sing. I just wept.

I would not have expected to have to go through all this in order for God to reveal to me my spiritual state. I recall 1 Samuel 16:7, when Samuel went to house of Jesse to anoint the future king of Israel. Samuel was thinking surely the first-born son was the chosen one, but God told Samuel not to look at the outward appearance because He looks at the heart. There's no denying it, we look at the outward appearance of things. Even in the church, we adopt a worldly mindset that rewards appearance and performance. God looks at the heart.

He had looked deeply into my heart and, with blunt honesty, said that He was pruning me. He did it through the most unsettling way imaginable, through a potentially fatal disease, in order to awaken me to my *real* infirmity. God used cancer to show me my spiritual HIV, and to say, "I want your heart in the secret places. I want your intimate fellowship, not your service or even your dedication."

This was a radical concept to a performance-driven Christian like me, who had been saved and indoctrinated into the performance-based Church of North America. In my performance mentality I had wandered off in a direction the Lord didn't want me to go, and in so doing I stumbled upon His true desire for His children. He wants our hearts. To capture mine, He revealed a cure for a virulent spiritual cancer, a cure that would open my eyes and propel me into His perfect love and true calling on my life.

# CHAPTER EIGHT
## The Cure

BACK IN MY HIGH SCHOOL DAYS and later at Auburn, during summers before fall practice, I'd prepare myself for the upcoming football season with a punishing physical workout regimen. On alternating days, I'd lift weights, run sprints, and do distance training. One day I'd lift weights until my muscles burned and then I'd strap on five-pound ankle weights and run a half-mile up the side of a mountain, following the power line towers to the top. About three-quarters up I'd stop and rest, and then sprint the rest of the way. By the summer's end I could almost make it to the top without stopping. Up on top, I'd sit on a favorite rock and gaze down on the valley below, catch my breath, and then I'd come racing back down the slope, slaloming in and out of the rocks.

On even days, I'd run different two-mile courses around our neighborhood in under twelve minutes, the standard time for fall practice. Then I'd head to the track and run ten 100-yard dashes. I credit this brutal regimen, repeated each day throughout the summer, for sending me back to Auburn each August in incredible shape. The coaches saw that I was ready and rewarded my effort with playing time and affirmation. They could see that my dedication had prepared me to perform to my full potential on the field.

That dedication and the results it produced reinforced what I had internalized since grade school: *everything* in our lives is performance-based. It's true in almost everything we do—athletics, education, job promotions, and even our relationships. From childhood our culture trains us to understand that we must perform or fall behind. It only gets worse as we get older. What's more, it's not all bad. The need to perform and do our best is how we maximize our human potential. It's just the way it is on this planet; it's an inescapable rule in the game of life on earth.

So how do we negotiate this simple fact of life as Christians? How do we transition from the world's performance-based mindset to a godly mindset, where nothing we can do apart from Christ can earn us God's salvation or favor?

Ephesians 2:8-9 says, "For it is by grace you have been saved through faith; and this not of yourselves, it is the gift of God, not by works, so that no one can boast" *(NIV)*. This word from God stands defiantly opposed to the worldly, man-centered mindset of North America. And we tend to view the Church as a sanctuary from a hyper-competitive, narcissistic culture. But what happens when the Church adopts the world's way of thinking? Christians view themselves as children of God, equipped with the Holy Spirit to resist and even conquer such carnal tendencies. We listen to sermons telling us we're free from the world's clutches and tell anyone who will listen that we serve an upside-down kingdom, unbound from the rules of this world. But do we really?

If most Christians today were asked to reconcile their biblical beliefs with their worldly attitudes and behaviors, I suspect most would be hard-pressed to do it. Sure, we know the truth, and read in the Word how man's wisdom and strength and his striving after perfection are utter foolishness in the eyes of God. Sermon after sermon warns against striving to earn God's love and favor, cautioning us that to do so will sabotage our spiritual growth. Yet, from my vantage, the church has bought into the world's ethos almost whole cloth, reinforcing the sad message that everything in our lives is indeed performance-based.

It's as if we live our lives like we're in a rowboat and act as if our spiritual success is determined by how hard we row. There's nothing wrong with rowing hard, but if we're rowing in our own strength, trying to earn our place in the boat, we're going to burn out and end up dead in the water. It has to be the Holy Spirit filling our sails and propelling us forward in His power. By the words we use with one another in our churches, I fear we're perpetuating a myth that, to live fully for Christ, we must row harder and harder. Matthew 6:33 tells us to seek first His righteousness and everything else will be added to our lives. We've developed a vast array of rowing techniques but have lost sight of Jesus.

## Rules for Worldly Success

The rules for worldly success have been hammered into us. They resound in our brains from the time we start preschool to the day we retire, confirming our worst suspicions that external criteria is the true measure of our worth. We're deemed by our fellow men as successes or failures, and we reflexively perform for one another in search of approval. It's the truth, and it's ingrained in us. It's how we've been trained to approach *everything*.

Isn't it odd that, by the sovereign miracle of God's love, we receive His salvation, accept adoption into His kingdom, learn that this world is not our true home, and yet still bring our quest for worldly trophies into this new life in the Spirit? It just proves how thoroughly we've been programmed.

Though the Bible dictates violently against it, believers need a standard by which their spiritual performance is judged. Much as they're trained to do in corporate America, they learn to compare themselves with their peers by the fervency of their prayers, service, and discipline.

These are all, of course, good things in the sense that diligence and good works are linked in the Word to our faith *(James 2:24)*. But in the same way that faith without works is dead, *works without faith is also dead*. I'm not talking about the blessing of a good works done at the Spirit's prompting, anointed from on high and in intimate fellowship with Christ and one's brothers. That's the invincible backbone of the authentic New Testament Christianity and something the world desperately needs more of. But I wonder how often good works done in Christ's name within the Body of Christ stem from a performance-based motive, driven by a need for external approval.

I've traveled this country and have seen it in church after church. Favor and promotion are granted to members by leadership based on who works the hardest and gets the most done. Some churches' entire leadership has been chosen this way. Again, not all bad, except when favor is granted for reasons divorced from one's depth of faith, holiness, or the demonstration of spiritual fruit and maturity. These are qualities that flow only from a red-hot, intimate relationship with Jesus and should be the measuring rod of one's spirituality. Rather, one's spirituality, not unlike a job performance review, is frequently judged by what one *does* rather than by who one *is* in Christ.

Works and good deeds, religious programs and activities, are all good and constructive and can certainly help advance the kingdom. Yet done from a wrong motive they amount to absolutely nothing, waste our time, and burn us out.

This should be Christianity 101, taught as a core principle in every church to new believers. But it is simply not put into practice in the Church today. Maybe we really don't believe it's true. Maybe we've come to a point in time where we don't truly trust what the Bible has to say on the subject. Look around—it doesn't take a genius to see that the spirit of this world has distorted, discredited, and falsely represented the Bible to the point that even many believers find themselves doubting that it's really true. When we lose faith in God's sovereign hand over our lives, in His miraculous economy, then it's dog eat dog. Performance is all that's left. It's much easier to do *stuff*.

So what's the answer? Where's the *cure*?

By now you probably see that it's going to require a dramatic rethinking in how we do church and approach the Lord of our salvation. It's going to require us to open our hearts—truly surrender our wills—to the Holy Spirit and let Him teach us how to "let go and let God." We need to invite the Holy Spirit back into our churches and plead with Him to teach us, because I'm afraid that there aren't many among us who have so embraced this teaching that they teach others. We've got to continually remind and encourage one another in this bedrock pillar of our faith: Jesus alone is our hope; He alone is the barometer by which we measure our spiritual standing before God.

By now many are probably thinking, *There's no way for me to live that kind of Christianity! I can't do it!* And guess what? You're absolutely right! There is no way to live the kind of passionate, intimate, victorious Christian life apart from the grace of God.

We live in a North American Christian culture in which the spiritual bar has been lowered to consist almost entirely of works. Christ's beautiful Church is filled with believers measuring themselves against a standard of mediocrity and rationalizing it all by thinking, *Well, at least I'm not doing what they're doing.* Jesus is no longer the bar, but our spiritual measuring stick is Mike, John, Susan, or Beth. *As long as I'm a cut above those other Christians, I'm good to go.*

Who are we kidding?

This struck home to me recently when a friend shared a conversation he had with the elder of a new church in his town. The church had lost members and faced some leadership challenges and, according to the elder, found itself searching for a "new identity."

"We need to come up with a 'brand,'" he told my friend, "that will set us apart from the other churches in the area. We need to be able to tell folks in one sentence what our church is about. Are we an evangelical outreach? Do we specialize in serving the needy? *We need an identity!*"

Do we really? I would argue instead that our identity is secure. It's in the Holy One of Israel, the Alpha and the Omega. Our identity is in the Lord of heaven and earth who has "hidden these things from the wise and learned and revealed them to little children" *(Matthew 11:25)*. That is "brand" enough, and more than we could ever possibly comprehend. If we abide in the Vine, we will emanate the aroma of Christ and do the works of Christ unmistakably and remarkably to the lost. Our service and good works will surge and flow as a natural act of worship ignited by His indwelling love. The Church, operating as an organic, relational Body of Christ, pursuing Jesus alone, does not need a branding campaign devised by marketing consultants. Jesus *is* the brand.

We cannot do it on our own. Only through God's grace is this possible.

## Paul Understood

The Apostle Paul says in 1 Corinthians 15:10: "But by the grace of God I am what I am, and His grace to me was not without effect. No, I worked harder than all of them—yet not I, but the grace of God that was with me."

Our Christian culture has sanitized this concept of grace into an almost passive ideal of benign mercy and forgiveness. It is much more than that. Let me be clear: sanctification, or the working out of one's salvation by God's grace as Paul mentions in the above verse, does not infer a lack of effort or a lack of labor on the part of believers. Sanctification by God's grace is a lack of *earning* and a lack of *deserving*. Grace does not turn us into a spiritual Jabba the Hut, enabling us to sit back, fat and lazy, and passively receive God's blessings. Sanctification does require a measure of effort, work, and labor as Paul points out, but it has to be Spirit-empowered and grace-motivated. Our labor is not to be based on *performance* in order to *earn* something but motivated by God's grace alone. Grace-motivated labor won't burn us out.

Go back to the verse. Paul begins with the acknowledgment that his identify and self worth, the fundamental framework of who is, is realized through "the grace of God." His focus is vertical, anchored not in human standards or comparisons but rooted firmly in the heavenly places. The grace Paul speaks of has nothing to do with human aspirations and ideals. To discern that which characterizes and motivates the Church today is to understand that this truth has been effectively lost. Paul's perspective comes not from a horizontal comparison with his first-century contemporaries but from the overwhelming realization that apart from God's grace he is *nothing*. Tell me, does that square with many of the teachings and practices seen in the church today? Does that square with all of those churches that chart their progress and success by the weekly offering, seat count, or signed commitment cards? These churches, led by dedicated, well-intentioned pastors and trustees, measure their success in the same way that Chrysler and GM measures theirs. I would suggest that there is no such thing as a bottom line in authentic, biblical Christianity.

"But Foster," you say, "I work hard for what I have. You don't understand. I can't depend on God's grace alone to sustain me. I have bills to pay, kids to put through college, a mortgage to serve. I have to *perform*."

Glad you brought that up, because Paul understood hard work. In the second part of verse ten he confesses that he "worked harder than all of them." He understood expending great effort and the need to provide for one's needs but wasn't enslaved to the rules of man's economy. The "all of them" refers to the other apostles, his peers, who together had spread out across the land preaching the gospel, building the Church, healing the sick, and raising the dead. Their combined effort resulted in tens of thousands getting saved. Theirs was hard, sweaty, clearly dangerous and difficult work, and Paul, more than anyone, understood and embraced the consistent, determined effort required to pull it off. Remember, he was the Pharisee of Pharisees, rigorously trained and steeped in the Jews' off-the-chart culture of performance and success. He understood that legalistic world better than any apostle.

Even so, he says that his efforts were not the result of his awesome work ethic but that every breakthrough had been "birthed" by the grace of God. In Colossians 1:29, he adds, "To this end I labor, struggling with all His energy, which so powerfully works in me." The word *struggling* here literally means "agonizing, straining to win a race." But whose energy is he tapping into? His own? No, *God's*! Paul labored from a place of intimate trust and *resting* in God's grace. This lifelong Pharisee, now filled with God's Spirit, was no longer laboring to demonstrate how skilled he was or hoping to gain promotion for his awesome evangelistic skills. His labor flowed from continual communication with his Lord, and from focusing his body, mind, and spirit on his relationship with Christ, listening for His voice, quieting his heart to hear the Spirit's soft whisper. Paul had, over time, trained his eyes to see what Jesus saw. Paul's rest came from the unspeakable peace of knowing that he couldn't do it himself. He needed and wanted God's grace.

Look out across the impoverished spiritual landscape of the Church of North America. What do you see? I'll tell you what I see: spiritual exhaustion and rampant burnout. Church leaders are walking away from ministry in droves because they've come to the end of their rope and don't know where to turn. Churches rise and fall in alternating bursts of feverish activity and spiritual stagnation as whole congregations suffer from that uniquely Christian syndrome of doing good things apart from God's presence. Rather allowing God's works to flow from His refreshing grace, they've jumped on the performance treadmill and are on the road toward burning out. They have the disease.

They don't understand that grace-motivated labor will not burn you out. Don't misunderstand: ministering in the power and anointing of the Holy Spirit *will* wear you out physically. You *will* work hard, in some cases harder than you've ever worked before. Ministering in the power and anointing of God is one of the most demanding and rewarding endeavors known to man. You will become physically and mentally tired, but in a good way, a fulfilling way, a *finishing-the-race-strong* way. Tired yes, but not swept into a deep fatigue of the soul.

These days, whenever I sense spiritual burnout, I can immediately tell that I've backslidden into that trap of performing in my flesh, fishing for man's approval rather than operating in a place of Spirit-led worship. It is a deep-rooted pattern perfected on the athletic fields of high school and college. I find immediate refreshment when I return my focus to God and surrender my agenda, confessing that I can do nothing apart from His grace.

As Christians, we can only grow in our faith by taking new steps into uncharted territory and wading out deeper into this new, mysterious ocean of possibility known as God's grace. Trust me, as you pursue this "grace truth" you will find yourself growing in faith, knowledge, and understanding. One day you will realize that you have been transformed in the hidden corridors of your performance-addicted soul. That's when you will become "the face for grace" for others. But first I need to share what I believe is the ultimate cure for the spiritual HIV I've seen ravaging the church. It's what I call "grace with blood on it."

# CHAPTER NINE
## Grace With Blood On It

WHEN I WAS A YOUNG CHRISTIAN, I had come to accept a fairly common spiritual picture of grace. It looked something like this: imagine that a storm is raging and you're treading water in the ocean, barely staying afloat. Land is nowhere in sight. As your strength gives out and you start to sink, God drops down from the sky and throws you a life preserver. You reach out and grab the life preserver and He pulls you to safety. By that act of God's undeserved grace, you are saved.

This is the scriptural symbolism for salvation that I learned in childhood and held on to throughout my early Christian life. I not only believed it but preached it for many years. I believe it's a picture of grace held by many in the Church of North America.

Yet through the years, as I grew in a greater revelation of God's Word through my bout with cancer and its messy aftermath, I gradually moved beyond this interpretation to what I believe is a more biblically accurate illustration. To do so, I refer to Ephesians 2:1-2: "As for you, you were dead in your transgressions and sins, in which you used to live when you followed the ways of this world and of the ruler of the kingdom of the air, the spirit who is now at work in those who are disobedient."

According to this verse in Ephesians, our salvation does not happen through a miraculous rescue while we are in the process of gradual death. It doesn't happen while we are treading water in the raging floodwaters, awaiting a life preserver and screaming for help at the tops of our lungs. This is a popular notion. But I believe the reality is that the unsaved are not treading water as the floodwaters rise; they are, in the most dramatic sense, already dead. Let me put it to you another way: when salvation arrives at our doorstep, we are already dead, rotting corpses, face down and butt up, bloated and stinking. Literally and figuratively, we are spiritual cadavers, deader than door nails.

Webster's defines *dead* as "deceased, departed, inanimate; without feeling, motion, or power, extinguished, extinct." That says it pretty well. We're lifeless lumps of sin-drenched carcass, without pulse, color, or respiration. The vultures are circling overhead and the crabs are nibbling at our flesh. When the life preserver splashed in the water beside us, we're unable to move much less raise a hand or utter a gasp for help. In this condition, need I even mention that we're completely unaware of our *need* for a Savior, incapable of crying out for forgiveness? We are not deeply in need, hopelessly troubled, or seriously imperiled; we are flat out *dead* in our sins. I think you get the picture.

I have a friend, a guy I've known for years who is not a Christian but someone with whom I've had countless opportunities to share Christ. What's interesting is that, as I've shared many different aspects of the Bible with him, he actually says he believes it all—that Jesus lived and died on a cross, and rose again. But when it comes to making a personal commitment to Christ, he doesn't get it. It's beyond his ability to comprehend his need for a Savior, and is, I believe, the perfect illustration of someone being absolutely spiritually dead. He doesn't think he needs a personal relationship with Christ. He thinks that he can be a good person and that's good enough. His spirit is dead to the truth. That's how we all are prior to the Holy Spirit's drawing of our hearts to Himself.

He (the Holy Spirit) is in complete control. God looks down on our putrefying spiritual flesh and touches us. Without so much as a nod of agreement from us, He breathes life into us, creating something radically new and original from moldering decay. Remember Ephesians: we were dead in our transgressions. He doesn't simply change our hearts or make our hearts different or somehow better. He gives us a "new" heart. *He gives us life!* Or, to paraphrase Ravi Zacharias: Jesus did not hang on a cross to make bad people good; Jesus hung on a cross to give dead people life.

I was recently at a youth conference at a Christian school in Georgia, talking to a young man about Jesus. He had no conviction whatsoever about any of it. I gave him a small booklet on John 3:16, explaining how God so loved the world that He gave His only begotten Son so that we might be saved. He still wasn't connecting, so I took out a piece of paper and drew it all out, breaking it down, illustrating not just that God loves us and desire to have a relationship with us, but how Jesus bridged the gap between sinful humanity and the holy Father through the cross. This young teenager's eyes glazed over and I could tell I wasn't getting through. A year later, I returned to that same school and ran into this young man again. To my complete surprise, he pulled me aside and told me that he kept returning to that pamphlet throughout the year and, all of a sudden, it made sense. He *got it*, and he gave his heart to the Lord. God had reached down and given him what he couldn't do for himself—He jump-started his heart to life.

Romans 3:10-11 explains it in a slightly different way. Paul points out that there is nothing good in us that we would ever pursue God, even when we're drowning in sin and in hopelessness: "There is no one righteous, not even one; there is no one who understands, no one who seeks God."

Left to our own human morality, blissfully ignorant and willfully defiant, we would all willingly hurl ourselves off the cliff into hell, grinning all the way down. That's the biblical picture of Ephesians 2:1-2. We're spiritually stillborn, birthed from the sin nature of Adam *(Romans 5:17)*, spiritually destitute, and morally inert. We have no ability to earn, posture ourselves, or even vaguely desire to seek or understand God's gift of salvation.

So let's get over it. Let's move beyond the sanitized notion of God's grace that we've been sold by the peddler's of a watered-down gospel. It's not the sterile definition of God throwing down a life preserver as we're sinking below the waves. What we need, rather, is a clear understanding of the profound gift of God's supernatural grace lifting us up from the grave amid our own septic and festering fluids.

In the next verses in Ephesians (2:8-9), we see the transaction in its enormity: "For it is by grace you have been saved, through faith—and this not from yourselves, it is the gift of God—not by works, so that no one can boast." Now examine that verse a bit closer. Ask yourself, to what does *this* in that verse rightly refer? It refers to God's dual gifts of grace and faith. Moreover, the verse tells us that the gift of faith flows *from* the gift of grace. So, even the very faith required for us to respond to the grace of His salvation is a God-given and initiated gift. He not only breathes life into a dead body, He animates our dry, bleached bones with faith activated by His grace. Once more for good measure: we are utterly and irredeemably spiritually unresponsive prior to salvation. Our redemption in Christ has been gifted to us supernaturally and undeservedly through God's grace, leading to faith unto salvation.

Can you see it? Jesus did not come to earth to make *bad* people *good*. He came to give *dead* people *life*. And, at the conclusion of the matter, what we all share is this: we're dead as fence posts, and what we need is the *life* only Jesus can give. We see this dramatically in Jesus' words to the woman at the well: "If you knew the gift of God and who it is that asks you for a drink, you would have asked Him and He would have give you living water" *(John 4:10)*. Jesus is our life giver. Life comes through Jesus alone, through His Holy Spirit.

Meditate on this for a few moments and let this reality begin to settle. As you fully realize the true gift of God's grace, waves of gratitude will begin to gush from every pore of your body. Trust me, I *know*. Like me, after my dramatic awakening following cancer surgery, your walk with God will be changed forever. Returning to church after my cancer surgery (I still had staples in my abdomen), waves of God's grace flowed over me during worship, and I could not quit crying.

It was the first step in my journey toward a full-throttled, biblical understanding of God's love for me. It thrust me forward to begin honoring Him with my life. It was a unilateral transaction that had nothing to do with my ability to rationalize or to receive His grace and everything to do with His unconditional, unfathomable love for me. Sadly, today's brand of Christianity has become so man-centered that we now believe—in what would appear to me to be in direct opposition to the Word of God—that God somehow needs our help in order to complete the salvation transaction. Jesus says in John 6:44 that, "No one can come to me unless the Father who sent me draws him, and I will raise him up at the last day." This Scripture reinforces Ephesians, which declares that unless and until God hooks His spiritual jumper cables up to the stone-dead battery of our hearts, we cannot be saved. Salvation begins and ends with Jesus—end of story. But the story is just beginning.

### The Bloody Cross

There's another illustration that I believe captures the essence of God's amazing grace in our Christian lives—a much grittier picture than most recognize. It's raw in ways that will make you squirm and may take you places you'd rather not go. This picture of grace requires something of us, altering the classic definition of "gift" as we might understand it. It's what I call "grace with blood on it," and it's the only way I know to reach an accurate understanding of how God works in our lives. For those who haven't a clue where I'm heading with this, this definition of grace is vividly portrayed in nearly every page of the Bible. It's a truth that penetrates to the core of our existence, yet most believers in mainstream Christianity not only fail to recognize this form of grace, they adamantly reject it.

Many have adopted instead a perverse and confused sense of the grace of God. How so? Well, we've already seen that salvation by God's grace is not a lack of effort by believers but a lack of *earning* and *deserving*. We've taken grace to mean an ever-flowing, bottomless cup of blessing. It's there in our devotionals and shouted constantly from the pulpit, training us to believe that most things in our lives, simply because we're Christians, should flow to us in a certain charmed alignment, blessings ever-rising in an uninterrupted arc of joy and blessing. Yes, we understand that we will experience trials and hardships and that these build our character and faith. Yet our unbiblical, entitlement mentality can lead us to expect that all suffering and unpleasantness will be mild-mannered and quickly resolved, lest we think that God has left us or forsaken us. It is this junk food brand of Christianity that causes some believers to despair when things don't turn out like they'd like, some even to the point of abandoning the faith.

But does this square with the Bible and its endless stories of faith and perseverance? God forbid that we would ever have to walk in the shoes of some of Christendom's great leaders. Take David, a "man after God's own heart." Do you remember the details of his life? After slaying Goliath and being anointed by the prophet Samuel as the next king of Israel, rising in the ranks to become one of Israel's most revered and decorated warriors, he was crowned king and lived happily ever after, right? No, he was reviled and rejected and forced into hiding by King Saul, the man for whom David had honorably served and repeatedly risked his life. Instead of loving David for his courage and faithfulness, out of jealousy Saul hated and hounded and chased David for fourteen years, several times to within an inch of David's life. Driven into the hills and caves, did David ever despair and complain to God? Yes, as a matter of fact, as we see throughout Psalms. Did he give up hope or lose faith in God? Never!

Ponder this for a moment: could it be, as we see in David's life, that what clearly appears to be the wrath of God is, in some cases, actually the grace of God? Let me say it another way: Could the grace of God look like the wrath of God to us sometimes? I say yes, and to prove it, I look no further than the cross. It's a perfect picture of the evident wrath of God working out the miracle of salvation of mankind. It is a bloody, raw picture of God's dreadful wrath working through Christ's grisly death and miraculous resurrection. What looked on the surface like a catastrophe was in fact God working an incredible, unspeakable act of grace for fallen mankind through His innocent Son.

Could this be true in our lives as well? Recall this verse from Jesus' own mouth: "The Son of Man must suffer many things and be rejected by the elders, chief priests and teachers of the law, and He must be killed and on the third day be raised to life" *(Luke 9:22).*

One verse later, He says, "If anyone would come after me, he must deny himself and take up his cross daily and follow me." Let's consider that passage, as well as the one that says, "Now if we are children, then we are heirs—heirs of God and co-heirs with Christ, if indeed we share in His sufferings in order that we may also share in His glory" *(Romans 8:17).*

The grace of God that saved mankind was won through suffering on the bloody, dirty, thorny cross. The grace that saved mankind was borne out of the Lord's torn, shredded and bleeding body as it hung on a cross, dying, lungs collapsing, and his body wracked with spasms of agony. Beyond the physical torture of the cross, our Lord's tender, pure heart had been broken by the sadistic rejection of those He had come to save. That, my friends, is grace with blood on it. Jesus, the very Son of God, Ruler of heaven and earth, was called the "Man of Sorrows." He walked a path of suffering that was as gritty and ugly and violent as anything we could imagine in our worst nightmares. It had the most dreadful of endings, or so it seemed for a time. For our salvation, Jesus endured an unspeakable, humiliating mockery and death.

I share this not to shock or upset but to simply remind an often sleek, proud, and entitled Church that this was, in fact, the path of our Lord. And it was also the path followed by Christ's disciples, and by generations of Christianity's early believers. It is the path laid out for all who choose to follow Him today, tempered with this promise: "And we know that in all things God works for the good of those who love Him, who have been called according to His purpose" *(Romans 8:28)*.

It is grace with blood on it—a glorious, supernatural grace often delivered through paths and means we would never choose on our own. It is a grace largely untaught in our Bible studies and Sunday schools, but which He has nonetheless provided to bring us fully into His fathomless joy and eternal salvation. This is the path we too have chosen, knowingly or otherwise.

Stories illuminating the "grace with blood on it" principle abound throughout the Bible. In Genesis 17 we read of Joseph, the talented, favored son of Jacob. Yet Joseph was despised by his brothers, thrown down into the pit, sold into slavery, falsely accused and left to languish in prison. Joseph, God's chosen ambassador for the salvation of millions, endured what must have felt like God's sneering wrath for thirteen years, each day confronted by desperate hardship and injustice yet knowing in his heart he was innocent. How many of us would have remained trusting and faithful through even one of these injustices? Yet Joseph endured and the Lord poured out a mighty blessing, imbuing him with supernatural gifts of wisdom and prophecy and then raising him up at the age of thirty-five to make him Pharaoh's right-hand-man.

Once again, *grace with blood on it*—an almost indescribable and unwarranted hardship handed down with no reason or explanation. To what end? God raining down grace in buckets? In our worldly context, we're tempted to read the story of Joseph with indignation and horror, wondering, *What did Joseph do to deserve that? What hidden sin must there have been in his life?* From what we can tell, God never offered an explanation, yet remained close to Joseph throughout, protecting and sustaining him, building him up, lavishing favor upon him and fine-tuning his character. What became of Joseph? We know the story. He ultimately found unimaginable redemption and promotion, experiencing God's richest blessing of grace—His grace *with blood on it.*

How many of us today, like Joseph, are willing to cling to God through seasons like these? Let's not even mention Job, who lost his family, fortune, and health in the very first chapter. Forty-one chapters later, God restores him to health and prosperity. Lucifer's plan was to see Job curse God and die. Yet from what appeared to be God's wrath flowed grace like a torrent, allowing Job to maintain his integrity, hold his tongue, and receive God's healing and restoration.

The stories are endless. Throughout the Book of Habbakuk, we see God's prophet verbally vomiting on God, demanding to know what God was doing and, more specifically, why He was doing it to *him.* Why was God using the wicked Assyrians to discipline His chosen (much holier) people? And he's spewing protests even as the Spirit of God is anointing him with incredible revelation to guide, instruct, and edify God's people for a thousand years into the future.

Grace with blood on it.

Some of you have experienced this truth personally. I tasted it in the midst of a battle with cancer that took me to new depths of panic and hopelessness. That season ended with God showering me in His powerful, penetrating love, melting my heart and drawing me toward an authentic understanding of His grace. For obvious reasons, this is not the message being preached today in most churches. It's not the message many of us want to hear. That's why I wrote this book—to help Christians to see this truth and to understand the true power of a life lived in the grace God has provided—a profound, unsearchable grace with blood on it.

Perhaps some can now begin to see how far off base we've strayed in our understanding of the truth of grace. Can we learn to receive and embrace the part of the Christian life stained with blood in order to go deeper and to get real with our Lord?

It isn't the tidy, compartmentalized Christianity with which many of us have grown accustomed. I'm speaking of the occasionally ugly, ragged, rawboned blood and sinew journey of walking alongside Christ in His sorrow and suffering. It's the triage test of walking alongside our brothers and sisters in their failures and sin, in their adulteries and addictions and abortions while lavishing them with God's acceptance, hope, and love. This isn't approving of or accepting each other's sin, but it's walking with one another, as Jesus does with us, exhorting, loving, teaching and lifting one another up, even in the smothering stench of our sin.

It brings to mind a scene in the movie *Passion of the Christ*, as Jesus scrawled with His finger in the dirt as men from the village aimed their rocks at a woman caught in adultery. When He had finished and the accusers had fled, He reached down and took hold of the hand of the prostitute, who moments earlier had been staring at death, about to be stoned by these men. It's a beautiful picture reminding us that, apart from His blood, apart from His grace, *that's us*. We are the prostitute. We are the whore that He rescues from certain death.

This is the path Jesus walks with us, extending His grace and ministering to the grotesque, loving the whores and prostitutes as well as the billionaire who has no idea that, despite having everything, he's lost.

This, for me, is the "face for grace" I spoke of earlier. It is the face of a bloody, bruised, and scarred people who have journeyed with the Lord in the darkened corridors of life. It is the face of those who have tasted how sweetly the Lord lavishes His love on His children in the midst of turmoil, fear, and pain.

# CHAPTER TEN
## A Face For Grace

NOT LONG AGO, I watched a documentary DVD of a true-life story that blew me away. It told the story of a family that experienced a heartbreaking tragedy. In it, a young mother was driving home and had just pulled her minivan off to the side of the road. Without warning, from the backseat, her four-year-old daughter unbuckled her seat belt and bolted out of the side door of the van. Before the mother had a chance to think about what was happening, the little girl darted out into the road, where she was hit by a car and was killed.

The other car didn't stop or slow down, leaving the mother screaming over her little girl. Days passed, and the hunt for the car that struck the little girl continued while the heartbroken mother and father mourned the loss of their child. The police continued the investigation and finally located the hit-and-run driver, but he was not the murderous monster everyone had envisioned. It turns out he was a close friend of the little girl's family, with a wife and children of his own. Moreover, he'd been the grateful recipient of this family's love, compassion, and Christ-like giving.

Asked why he didn't stop after hitting the girl, the man was stunned and had no idea that he'd struck a child. He thought he'd simply hit a bump in the road. This somehow intensified the tragedy, involving a close family friend who would now certainly go to jail for a crime he wasn't even aware he'd committed. The entire community was aware of the closeness of these two families. But no one expected what happened next.

At the funeral, the child's family insisted that the driver and his family sit with them on the front row. Afterwards, the girl's father appeared before the state's Supreme Court to appeal to the judges to spare his friend criminal charges. The court consented, and a short time later the girl's family, along with many others from the town, helped to build the man's family a new home to replace the crumbling structure in which they lived. Today, both families remain the best of friends, even as the mother and father still mourn for their little girl.

To most of us, a story like this doesn't even make sense. In interviews for this documentary, many townspeople could not put into words what they had witnessed, so astonished were they at how everything turned out. The grace shown by this family left the entire town speechless. Watching the mom and dad lose their beloved daughter in a tragic accident was heart-wrenching, but to see them reach out in love to the man who killed her short-circuited every preconception they held about how humans react to tragedy. This rare Christian husband and wife had offered to a watching world a powerful portrait of Christian grace, writing an unexpectedly hope-filled ending to a nightmare. To the cynical observers of their hometown, it looked strange indeed, an obvious "God thing" playing out in their midst. By story's end an entire town had been swept up in a real-life parable of the forgiveness and restoration that can come only through Christ. Through this remarkable mother and father, the town touched and tasted Jesus, witnessing in the process something seldom seen—an authentic "face for grace."

The story left me asking myself how this magnificent truth—this incomparable *face for grace*—can be restored to a Christian culture obsessed with appearance and performance. How can it be translated when the process, polish, and appearance of spiritual activity has become, in many cases, more important than intimately knowing the person of Jesus? In such a performance-oriented culture, how can we begin to live in such a way as to present a bona fide "face for grace" to the world? I believe it's only possible as we read and immerse our-selves in the Word and learn from the average men and women God has used and refined and molded through the ages. Let's allow Scripture to be our anchor in this. The Bible offers us countless examples of men and women, clearly flawed servants of God, working out an otherworldly selflessness—even a supernatural face for grace—when confronted by desperate, even death-defying circumstances. Let me ask you a question. Have you ever been relentlessly pursued by someone with a mind to do you bodily harm? I have. At least I've dreamt that I have, in a recurring dream that has subjected me to many restless nights. In it, I'm being pursued by someone who wants to capture me and put me in jail for the rest of my life. I often wake up in cold sweats, thinking that life as I've known it is over and convinced I'm going to spend the rest of my days in jail. What it has given me, I believe, is a realistic feeling of what it must feel like to be chased and hunted, potentially to the death, like in a scene from a horror movie.

David knew well the feeling of being chased and hunted for no apparent reason. We read about it in 1 Samuel, how this anointed, courageous, godly young man, having defended Israel's honor by slaying Goliath and rising to the status of a national war hero, found himself relentlessly pursued by King Saul. Driven to the edge of insanity over jealousy of David, Saul ignored David's faithful service, put a bounty on his head and hunted him to within an inch of his life. I doubt many of us can imagine the profound stress and fear this would create, running for one's life, hiding in caves, trying to stay a step ahead of the guy with the scope and rifle aimed at your head.

In 1 Samuel 24:1-22, we see David in full flight from King Saul, who, interestingly, David never stops acknowledging as Israel's God-anointed king. It was David's acknowledgment of unwavering respect for God's chosen, in fact, that made his predicament all the more perplexing. Saul had mustered 3,000 fighting men in the desert of En

Gedi and was hot on David's heels. When the entire regiment arrived at the cave where David and his men were hiding, it seemed that God had delivered Saul into their hands and that David's running would soon be over.

David's response should have been a no-brainer—sneak up on Saul and put him to sleep permanently. The temptation to take matters into his own hands and relieve his suffering must have been off-the-charts. But David's grace response kicked in, and he gave Saul exactly what he *didn't* deserve. David sneaks up, cuts off a corner of Saul's robe and, as his enemy rides away, cries out to tell the whole world that he had just spared Saul's life.

David had provided a face for grace for King Saul, and it had a powerful impact. Saul wept aloud, and confessed to David, "You are more righteous than I. You have treated me well, but I have treated you badly" *(1 Samuel 24:16-17).*

I wonder how this impacted David's hard-core warriors, the men who had been hiding with him in caves. All we know is that they went on to legendary feats of courage and an unbeaten string of victories, fighting for God's glory and for Israel's honor with unmatched zeal. They had all witnessed David's face for grace, and I'm sure they never forgot it.

Now let's fast-forward to a modern day example. Remember the Los Angeles riots in the early 1990s following the Rodney King verdict? Like many, I watched the rioters on TV running amok and burning down L.A.'s inner city after the police charged in King's beating were acquitted. Yet one face from that episode remains fixed in my memory—a truck driver by the name of Reginald Denny. Mr. Denny's timing wasn't the greatest. He happened to be driving his truck through the heart of the worst rioting when a bunch of thugs pulled him from his cab and began beating him with kicks and bricks. As the helicopters hovered overhead, viewers witnessed a savage mauling. One kid ran up to Mr. Denny and smashed him in the skull with a large brick.

Denny survived terrible injuries to his head and body. Video footage helped police identify and convict his assailants, yet as the trial reached its conclusion, Mr. Denny took a moment to speak. What he said stunned the world. He forgave his attackers and said he held no ill will toward them. The country's collective jaw dropped. *Everyone*—the media, police, commentators, civilians—took notice. News commentators went on about it for weeks. Beaten to within an inch of his life, Reginald Denny chose to forgive and became a face for grace for all who heard him that day, especially his attackers.

We've talked about Joseph, a young boy who showed early promise but saw his hopes dashed. He was his father's pride yet a source of disdain to his brothers, who threw him in a well and sold him into slavery. In Egypt, having served his master with honor, he was falsely accused and thrown in prison for roughly thirteen years, sitting in the dark, filthy cell, year after year, daily confronted with how his early promise had turned to ashes. Like David, he had every reason to surrender to bitterness, anger, and unforgiveness. *But he didn't.* Joseph submitted to the Holy Spirit and allowed the Lord to keep his heart soft during his long imprisonment, faithfully completing every menial job given him, honing his prophetic gifting, listening to the Holy Spirit, and ministering to his fellow prisoners and probably even the guards.

Confronted years later by the brothers who had sold him into slavery, Joseph, now Pharaoh's right-hand man, demonstrated one of the Bible's heroic examples of forgiveness. Listen to his words from Genesis 45:4-8: "Then Joseph said to his brothers, 'Come close to me.' When they had done so, he said, 'I am your brother Joseph, the one you sold into Egypt! And now, do not be distressed, and do not be angry with yourselves for selling me here, because it was to save lives that God sent me ahead of you.'"

Years later, after their father Jacob had died, Joseph's brothers, terrified that he might finally exact a much-deserved revenge, asked, "What if Joseph holds a grudge against us and pays us back for all the wrongs we did to him?" But in verses 10-21 we see that Joseph was merciful to the end: "Don't be afraid. Am I in the place of God? You intended to harm me, but God intended it for good to accomplish what is now being done, the saving of many lives. So then, don't be afraid. I will provide for you and your children. And he reassured them and spoke kindly to them."

Allow a moment for this story to soak into your hearts. Meditate on this act of mercy and grace so you don't miss what God has for us in this story—a beautiful face for grace communicating God's enduring love, mercy, and forgiveness to a sin-wracked world.

David's and Joseph's actions fly in the face of their cultures and ours. They chose a course that was and is radically countercultural in every respect. It is what Jesus did in dying on a cross for our sins. It is what God expects of His Church. Yet the fact remains that, whether inside or outside the walls of the Church, we see and experience very little of this other-centered, grace-saturated behavior. The Reginald Dennys of this world are few and far between. At its bedrock core, grace is an otherworldly phenomenon. It defies human nature; it defies culture. It is God-breathed.

Some years back, a close friend of mine emerged from a very legalistic system of "doing" church. It was obvious to me, not because he was abrasive or crass but because, as I sought to get to know him and spoke of God's grace in my own life, I'd get the thousand-foot stare. He didn't get it, even though he instinctively knew that grace was what he wanted and needed. Yet like so many of us, he didn't know how to get there. Over the last five years I have watched as the Holy Spirit has done an amazing work in this man's life. Today I can see that he no longer responds legalistically to spiritual challenges but with a wisdom grounded in a personal knowledge of God's grace. Today he is mentoring other men in the countercultural truths of grace, ensuring, as did Joseph and David in their day that a second generation face for grace would shine to the world.

If you're fortunate enough to be given a chance to be a face for grace for those in your domain, be prepared for a powerful response. The Scriptures say that Saul wept in response to David's radical expression of extreme grace. True expressions of grace elicit strong reactions. Saul was completely overwhelmed by David's overt expression of grace. Joseph could not contain his own emotions as he lavished grace on his brothers. Genesis 45:2 tells us that "he wept so loudly that the Egyptians heard him and Pharoah's household heard about it." That uncontrolled emotion came from being a face for grace under extreme conditions.

David and Joseph, by giving their adversaries what they *didn't* deserve, literally stopped time, altered the atmosphere, and changed history.

Every now and then, I get an opportunity to be a face for grace in my own small way. Just a few days ago, my wife Laura and I walked into the gym to work out. From the corner of my eye I saw a guy at the back of the gym turn and literally run toward us. Before I could say anything, this fellow came at me with tears streaming down his face and wrapped me in a bear hug that nearly cracked a rib. He was a guy I knew who'd been in a tough season of life. He'd recently endured a second divorce, lost a job he loved, and watched as custody of his children was stripped from him. He knew he'd made bad choices that caused much of the pain, but his sense of abandonment from the people he thought were his friends broke his heart.

As tempting as it might have been to turn our backs on his messy situation, Laura and I made a conscious choice to be a face for grace for this man. When every move he made offended others and buried him deeper in a hole of his own making, we stood by him. Our expectations were low, but the results amazed us. This friend of ours is now in a new job and is getting his life squared away. More importantly, he has been ministering to others. While making a delivery to a local hospital my friend was told that he had helped someone turn his heart back toward God. Being a face for grace is a contagious thing. It's in our power to choose, and in so doing, pass it along to a second generation.

# CHAPTER ELEVEN
## Broken Cisterns

I RECENTLY GAVE A TALK to a group of high school seniors. It was a message on Jeremiah 2:11-13 that I believe speaks to modern day Christians just as it did to ancient Israel: "Has a nation ever changed its gods? (Yet they are not gods at all.) But my people have exchanged their Glory for worthless idols. Be appalled at this, O heavens, and shudder with great horror," declares the Lord. "My people have committed two sins: They have forsaken me, the spring of living water, and have dug their own cisterns, broken cisterns that cannot hold water."

If I were to attempt to draw a picture of the Church of North America using contemporary terms and rhetoric, none of it would come nearly as close to describing our plight as these stark words from Jeremiah. The essence of what I've been saying can be boiled down into these few words: "They have forsaken me, the spring of living water, and have dug their own cisterns, broken cisterns that cannot hold water."

For the most part, I believe the Church today is essentially doing its own thing, spinning its wheels on an unbiblical treadmill of "activity"—programs, busyness, and often trivial, empty spiritual-looking exercise. Much of it is being done in the name of Christ and is, almost uniformly, being done for good reasons according to our human standards. But I fear that the sum total of all this activity is that we are digging broken cisterns and forsaking God, the spring of living water.

In our working and trying and striving to do some little good in our own corners of the world for Jesus Christ, we're wearing thin and burning out. Why? Because we're devoid of His presence in our midst. We're doing our own thing for good reasons in our own strength, motivated by high ideals yet, too often, independent of God and inexcusably without His Spirit. I liken it to a football team driving down the field, exerting themselves, working hard, doing their best to score against a tough opponent but with their star quarterback sitting on the sidelines in street clothes. Like Martha of the New Testament, we're often reduced to scurrying about looking for things to keep us busy when what we really need to be is Mary, lingering long at the feet of Jesus and drinking lavishly of His presence, availing ourselves of His Spirit, and ministering to one another in His genuine anointing. How is it that we've forgotten as a Church what it truly means to draw near to our first love, to be genuinely grafted into the Vine? Our ears have become deaf to His voice, so how can we assume to be about His business, doing only what our Father tells us? We've forgotten!

From my vantage, the Church of North America is forever driving up the field, frantically rifling passes into the flat, running draw plays up the middle, doing all the stuff she has been taught to do to win the game, hoping and praying for victory—but having left God on the bench. We're building our own cisterns, busily, pragmatically, programmatically pursuing the prize, guided by our books and manuals, business plans and growth charts, but—I mean no disrespect, but please hear me on this—*God is not involved!* He's nowhere to be found because we've sprinted off down the path without Him, drained of our lifeblood, forsaking our spring of living water.

Is it any wonder that Christianity's influence on our culture is disappearing, and that trends show we are in danger of losing the next generation of Christians to the culture? Is it any wonder that our President, emboldened by the weight of statistics supporting him, declares to the world that the United States is no longer a Christian nation even though our history, culture, laws, and traditions have from our very founding been profoundly influenced by Christianity? I'm certainly not the first to say or observe it; you've undoubtedly been punched in the face by the two-by-four of society's postmodern slide into secularism. But the Church has allowed itself to become infected with the world rather than infecting the world for Jesus.

We're blessed in this country that, in many communities, there's a church on almost every corner. Yet are we one as Jesus and the Father are *(John 17:11)*, or is each church building it's own little kingdom? Have we, as Jesus added, been "brought to complete unity to let the world know that You have sent Me, and have loved them even as You have loved me" *(John 17:23)*? Of course not. Many churches are competing against the church across the street for members, each establishing its own "brand," building its own Tower of Babel, trying to reach heaven through its own cleverness and industry. Sure, we're all trying to be nice, friendly Christian folks, acting how we think devout believers ought to act when, in fact, our hearts are far from God. Worse, we've become numb to His presence. Just as in the days of Jeremiah, we've built our own cisterns that do not and cannot hold His springs living water.

Please hear me, my friends. I am not trying to be negative or critical about the Church. I am just trying to be truthful about what I've seen. It took a cataclysmic health crisis to help me see and understand what has become my life's message. This is what I see when I am out ministering among the churches. Time is short, and we must quit pretending that all is well when in fact we're bleeding to death. It's time to quit consoling ourselves with empty rhetoric and worldly strategies that amount to putting a band-aid on a grenade wound. I have no agenda in writing this other than to be faithful to Jesus my Lord. The local church is the Body and Bride that Christ established to minister to the world, and we're not doing it.

A doctor sat me down and looked me in the eye and said the word "cancer," and that one word spiritually stripped me naked, snapped me awake, and peeled the scales off my eyes. It took that shock of my own mortality to usher me into the reality of His grace. And, let me tell you, friends, it wasn't a safe, sanitized grace. Rather, it was a grace with blood splattered all over it, with sores and scabs and broken bones and fainting flesh and trembling hearts. It's the biblical kind of grace that David and Joseph and Jonah experienced in their hurricane winds, heartbreaking upheavals, and nightmare betrayals of life; the kind of grace that allows God to reveal His love and power in the midst of darkness and show Himself, as His Word unequivocally declares, to be King and Lord of the universe, the One who delivers us from them all. If it took surviving cancer and subsequent years of God's discipline, kneading, and molding to tenderize my heart and cause me to pursue the person of Jesus rather than church activity, then praise the Lord. It was the only way forward, the only cure for my condition. It opened my eyes and enabled me to see that I had, with the best of intentions, ignorantly and subconsciously forsaken my first love for a lie.

## The Lord is Tasty

Anne Graham Lotz, Billy Graham's daughter, has developed a powerful ministry of her own and has spoken frankly of her childhood disillusionment with the Church. I read an interview recently in which she recalled being raised in a church culture lacking in love and true spirituality while overflowing with judgment and pettiness. Somewhat ironically, it was this background, growing up in a church community influenced (if not dominated) by the personality and preaching of her famous father, that showed her how Christians have been indoctrinated into believing that their spiritual lives begin and end by being saved and attending church.

"That's such a shallow understanding," she said, addressing what most Christians accept as core doctrine. "A relationship can begin at church, but it can't end there. Being a Christian is a personal relationship with God, a thriving relationship based on communication."

The critical problem among today's community of believers, she observed, is that far too many are "too reliant" on the church and "have fallen into a convenient pattern of allowing their church experience to be their sum total of experiencing God." The Sunday-only mentality that defines the typical Christian's spiritual depth, Lotz suggested, leaves them ill-equipped to ride out the storm when church and their fellow Christians inevitably disappoint them. How strong would your relationship with God be, she asked, "if you could no longer go to church, or were homebound and lost your friends at church?" And then she shared an insight that hit me in the chest like a 300-pound nose tackle: "Christians today are carrying on a love affair with the Bible, rather than pursuing and falling into a love relationship with Jesus Christ."

In that one sentence she nailed one of the most subtle symptoms of spiritual HIV disguised as authentic spirituality. We read our Bibles, maybe even memorize verses. That's awesome—fantastic— but not if it ends there; not if God's not involved, not if the Holy Spirit is not breathing life into the pages and whispering invigorating mysteries into our souls.

"Taste and see that the Lord is good; blessed is the man who takes refuge in Him" *(Psalm 34:8, NIV)*. My friends, the Lord is *savory*; He is delectably flavorful and good. When you have tasted the incredible richness of the Lord in prayer, in worship, in quietude, and in service, you know it.

The stale bread of rote, man-centric, appearance-driven, performance-based church activity is little more than a recipe for spiritual burnout. It is no substitute for the energizing, spine-tingling, hot, and spicy green chili afterburn of His savory presence.

Do not misunderstand. I am not in any respect speaking against reading our Bibles. God forbid! John 1:14-15 calls Jesus the living Word: "The Word became flesh and made His dwelling among us."

The Bible is absolute, inerrant truth, our guidebook into a deeper knowledge of God. It is a lamp unto our feet to comfort us, teach us, convict us of sin, and lead us on the paths of righteousness. But can we carry on an intimate personal relationship with the Bible? Of course not, just as we can't truly get to know the person of Jesus by simply interjecting ourselves into well-meaning programs and church activity. Yet when we are working intimately with Jesus, divinely motivated by His Word, we "can do all things through Christ who strengthens me" *(Philippians 4:13, NKJ)*.

Reading, knowing, and cherishing God's Word is critical to a proper understanding of God and His truth, but it is not a substitute for knowing and loving Jesus. By the same token, by seeking our "God experience" through church attendance, Bible reading, or service in the name of Jesus but *without* Jesus and *absent* His Holy Spirit, we ignore the admonition of Proverbs 24:27: "Finish your outdoor work and get your field ready; after that, build your house." The true work of the Church is to do whatever it takes, and however long as it takes, to press into God's presence with all of our hearts, minds, and strength. Whatever flows naturally from that "field work" will last. It will not burn. It is eternal.

Brothers and sisters, we're building our own cisterns, worshipping our own idols, and forsaking our spring of living water. Simply put, we're sinning. We're holding God's name up to emptiness, having unwittingly traded the focus on God to a focus on man. We've shifted from a divine focus on God to fooling ourselves into thinking we can manufacture something that only God can manufacture—the pure harvest that flows only from His presence in our midst! These broken cisterns are the local church.

I'm speaking of what I see. We're in dire straits. At a time in history in which the world desperately needs a strong, vibrant, Spirit-filled Body of Christ, we're instead weak, carnal, and worldly. We can complain all we want as the world steamrolls toward hell, yet because we've missed Him, we're demonstrating to the lost that we're really no different.

Prayers are being uttered, Scripture is being read, ministry is technically taking place in our churches, but too much of it is a parched landscape, a dry, mechanical drill. Our pastors argue fine points of doctrine, and we debate theology until we're blue in the face, and for what? While there are always exceptions, one has to ask how much of what's taking place in the hearts and minds of believers is eternal?

## Face for Grace to Future Generations

God's transcendent grace is here to show us the way if we are open to receiving it. It isn't the safe, sanitized, flowery definition of grace. It is a grace that reveals itself in power and intimacy yet, as chronicled throughout the Bible, felt most powerfully amid turbulence and transition, during life's tremors and storms. It is a rule of Scripture, in fact, that more often than not, we run headlong into trouble as we delve deeper into our relationship with God. It's why the Church is mired in mediocrity. We have become lazy, comfortable, and believe ourselves to be entitled to the mammon of this world. Yet the Lord is waiting for us in the deep, eternal realms. This "grace with blood on it" is our Lord revealed in His raw, breathtaking reality. If we will yield ourselves to this grace as we travel in His deeper realms of intimacy, He will teach us the mysterious beauty of His divine purpose in our lives.

This is not merely my opinion or some obscure, theological perspective—it is biblical truth, dramatically revealed on most every page of the Bible through the stories of His servants.

So how do we allow this truth of grace to deepen its root system in our lives? How can we become a face for grace to future generations? I sense some of these truths are found in Titus 2:11-15. Paul writes to Titus, his friend in ministry: "For the grace of God that brings salvation has appeared to all men." Simply put, we need the *grace* of God to get a fresh *vision* of God. We see and feel grace in the person of Christ. The gospel resonates with the story of grace. It is this story that converts us from seeing God as being merely useful and convenient to meet our ends to being seen as He truly is—awesome, majestic, the One and only.

As we've seen time and time again, our performance-based, consumerism approach to "doing" church often causes us to approach God as the great ATM machine in the sky, our means to an end, our celestial advocate devoted to moving our agenda forward. If we have the guts to admit it to ourselves, the majority of the time *we're* the focus. What we do in the name of Jesus is too often done for the advancement of *our* causes, our good works undertaken for the enhancement of *our* reputations. John the Baptist said of his relationship to Jesus: "He must become greater; I must become less" *(John 3:30)*. Grace in Christ, the person of Jesus, must be our focus.

I wonder if we have almost passed the point at which we can even stir our hearts to recall what it is to be authentically "other-focused" in the biblical sense. In this threatening economic environment, for example, I wonder how many Christians would be willing to risk upsetting their carefully constructed illusion of material security in order to approach Jesus more intimately, truly put their trust in God, and relate to one another in a more authentic fashion.

If we are to become a face for grace to others, it's going to require a drastic reversal of our corporate church attitudes. It will require each of us to take a serious accounting of ourselves, and, by the power of Jesus Christ, to prepare ourselves to live a different, grace-filled life. It will require us to embrace the principle of grace with blood on it, to walk closely with our Lord, and to refuse to exchange our spring of living water for cracked, broken, manmade cisterns.

This grace I'm talking about is the only thing that will enable us through Christ to live the life of a disciple, and to live the abundant life *above* this world. It's the only thing that will empower us to be joyful in the face of utter hopelessness and, more importantly, to project hope to others. This grace I'm talking about is the only thing that will allow us, the *Church*, with hope and trust transcending trial and circumstance, to weather the storms to come. It's the only thing that will help us face and defeat the giants that would otherwise terrify and overwhelm us, even as our neighbors, leaders, and government run for cover. The grace of God in Jesus Christ, dear Church of North America, is what we must put our hope in. Not our programs, clever though they may be; not in our effort and industriousness, vigorous though we may be. It's where we must put our focus. For if we allow the Goliaths that mock our God to be our focus, there is no hope; if we allow the economy which threatens to crumble about us to be our focus, we have no hope; if our government, or the President, or Wall Street, or health care or social security become our focus, then we *really* have no hope. If we allow whatever dire circumstances may come to become our focus, then we have no hope. To even begin to consider the possibility of achieving this, we've got to be willing as a Body, moving forward in ranks, to take our eyes off of this world and focus them squarely on to our Lord Jesus and His kingdom.

*And never take our eyes off of Him!*

Titus 2:11-15 tell us that the grace of God that brings salvation "teaches us to say no to ungodliness and worldly passions and to live self-controlled, upright, and godly lives in the present age while we wait for the blessed hope—the glorious appearing of our great God and Savior, Jesus Christ, who gave Himself for us to redeem us from all wickedness and to purify for Himself a people that are His very own eager to do what is good. These, then, are the things you should teach.  Encourage and rebuke with all authority."

The language in these verses is of a substitutionary nature. Christ took our place. The word *redeem* means "to pay the price." The debt and the price He paid is one of infinite nature. The infinite Christ paid the infinite price to "purify a people that are His very own" *(Titus 2:14)*. We can only understand our need for His grace as we worship Him, praise Him, pray to Him in a constant process of repentance.

Christ loves us and He purifies us for Himself. It is God's grace that encourages me, convicts me, and empowers me to be eager to do what is good and to obey Him. It is His grace that frees me to march into the storms of life fearlessly, knowing it is there in the tail of the twister, that His strength is greatest, that His love is most apparent. My motivation for obedience comes in the constant awareness of His grace and is animated by the understanding that I am forgiven.

His grace frees me to fully embrace His love for me. Jesus is my Savior, the substitutionary recipient of my sin and its punishment. I am forgiven. I can come back to God in repentance. I don't need to earn His forgiveness. I am already forgiven.

Do you hear that Church of North America? You are forgiven. Grace is your inheritance. This is the raw essence of God's love for us. It is His supernatural grace worked out with fear and trembling through trial and circumstances, enlivening us, strengthening us, and training us, for eternity.

## ACKNOWLEDGEMENTS

Thank you, David Halbrook, for your help in crafting and shaping this project. Without your expertise and patience, we would have never made it! You have become a dear brother through this process. Meaghan Locklear, your cover designs are awesome! Thanks for using *His* talents for *His* glory. Thank you "Clemson girls" for your thoughts while we sat in our den developing the "ground floor" ideas for the cover. Ann-Marie and Lolly, your suggestions all the way through have been so valuable. I am enjoying watching you grow in His grace. Continue to pursue Jesus. Thank you to my Band of Brothers and Sisters at KBM who always have my back in prayer. Laura, my wife, you are so faithful to pray and encourage. You are the greatest! Thank you prayer team and financial supporters, who, for over 17 years have so faithfully enabled me to stay on the front lines and continue to fight the good fight.